SCHOLASTIC

100 Task Cards

Context Clues

Reproducible Mini-Passages With Key Questions to Boost Reading Comprehension Skills

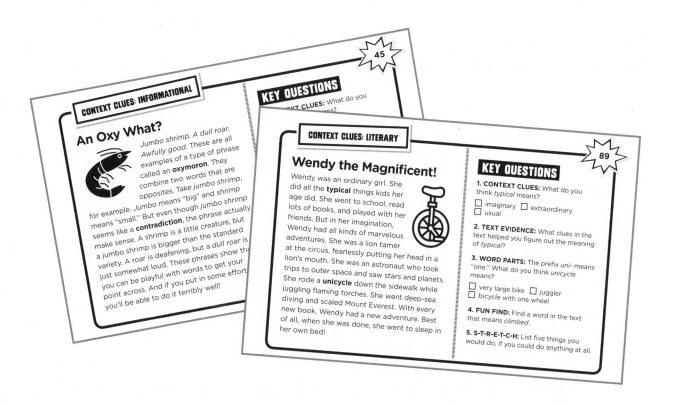

CONTEXT CLUES: INFORMATIONAL

An Oxy What?

Jumbo shrimp. A dull roar. Awfully good. These are all examples of a type of phrase called an **oxymoron**. They combine two words that are opposites. Take *jumbo shrimp*, for example. *Jumbo* means "big" and *shrimp* means "small." But even though *jumbo shrimp* seems like a **contradiction**, the phrase actually make sense. A shrimp is a little creature, but a jumbo shrimp is bigger than the standard variety. A roar is deafening, but a *dull roar* is just somewhat loud. These phrases show that you can be playful with words to get your point across. And if you put in some effort you'll be able to do it terribly well!

CONTEXT CLUES: LITERARY

Wendy the Magnificent!

Wendy was an ordinary girl. She did all the **typical** things kids her age did. She went to school, read lots of books, and played with her friends. But in her imagination, Wendy had all kinds of marvelous adventures. She was a lion tamer at the circus, fearlessly putting her head in a lion's mouth. She was an astronaut who took trips to outer space and saw stars and planets. She rode a **unicycle** down the sidewalk while juggling flaming torches. She went deep-sea diving and scaled Mount Everest. With every new book, Wendy had a new adventure. Best of all, when she was done, she went to sleep in her own bed!

KEY QUESTIONS   45

KEY QUESTIONS   89

1. CONTEXT CLUES: What do you think *typical* means?
- [ ] imaginary [ ] extraordinary
- [ ] usual

2. TEXT EVIDENCE: What clues in the text helped you figure out the meaning of *typical*?

3. WORD PARTS: The prefix *uni-* means "one." What do you think *unicycle* means?
- [ ] very large bike [ ] juggler
- [ ] bicycle with one wheel

4. FUN FIND: Find a word in the text that means *climbed*.

5. S-T-R-E-T-C-H: List five things you would do, if you could do anything at all.

New York • Toronto • London
Auckland • Sydney • New Delhi • Hong Kong

Passages written by Carol Ghiglieri and Justin Martin
Cover design by Tannaz Fassihi
Cover photo © Fertnig/Getty Images
Interior illustrations by The Noun Project

ISBN: 978-1-338-60317-0

Scholastic Inc., 557 Broadway, New York, NY 10012
Copyright © 2020 by Scholastic Inc.
Published by Scholastic Inc.
All rights reserved. Printed in the U.S.A.
First printing, January 2020.

2 3 4 5 6 7 8 9 10   40   26 25 24 23 22 21

CONTENTS

INTRODUCTION

Welcome to *100 Task Cards: Context Clues!*

Reading comprehension is essential. When students understand a wide variety of informational and literary texts, it helps them learn new skills, make sense of history, develop critical thinking, enjoy works of fiction, and succeed at standardized tests. And a key part of that understanding rests on their ability to effectively use context clues.

What are context clues? Simply stated, they are *the clues readers use to figure out the meaning of unknown words encountered in texts*. These clues can take many forms, including definitions, examples, and antonyms. And they require the trained eye of a reading detective to spot them. Consider, for example, these two sentences: *Bats are **nocturnal**. Bats sleep during the day, hanging upside down.* A reader adept at context-clues sleuthing would be able to glean that nocturnal means *active at night* because that is the opposite of *active during the day*. Sound like a tricky ability for kids to acquire? Indeed, it is.

But don't despair. *100 Task Cards: Context Clues* is here to help your students master this critical skill in just minutes a day! Each card includes an informational or literary mini-passage along with key questions that give students plenty of practice unlocking the meaning of new words by using these six types of context clues:

* **Definition**
* **Example**
* **Synonym**
* **Antonym**
* **Inference**
* **Word Parts**

The cards are designed for instant use—just photocopy them and cut them apart, and they're good to go. The cards are also designed for flexible use. They're perfect for seatwork, centers, or meaningful homework. They're also great for independent practice or for work with partners, small groups, and even the whole class.

The questions on the cards will help students hone critical comprehension skills they'll rely on for a lifetime. And here's more good news: Because the mini-passages were written by professional authors with a gift for engaging young readers, kids will absolutely *love* them!

So what are you waiting for? Read on for tips that will help your students grow into confident, fluent, "deep" readers—quickly and painlessly. And don't forget to look for the other great *100 Task Cards* books in this series, including *Informational Text, Literary Text, Text Evidence, Making Inferences,* and *Figurative Language.* The kids in your class will thank you.

TEACHING TIPS

About the 100 Context Clues Task Cards

This book contains 100 context clues cards, each with a mini-passage; 50 feature informational text and 50 feature literary text. The texts vary by topic and tone to give students a rich variety of reading material that correlates with current state standards. (For a list of the standards these cards address, see page 9.) Each card presents five key questions.

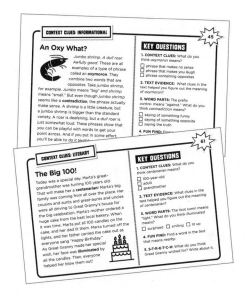

1. **Context Clues:** This question challenges students to use context clues to define an unknown word in the passage.

2. **Text Evidence:** This question challenges students to cite the text evidence they used to arrive at that word's definition.

3. **Word Parts:** This question challenges students to use a root word to glean the meaning of a second unknown word in the passage.

4. **Fun Find:** This question challenges students to use a definition to locate a third unknown word in the passage.

5. **S-T-R-E-T-C-H:** This question challenges kids to boost creative and critical-thinking skills by responding to a motivating prompt.

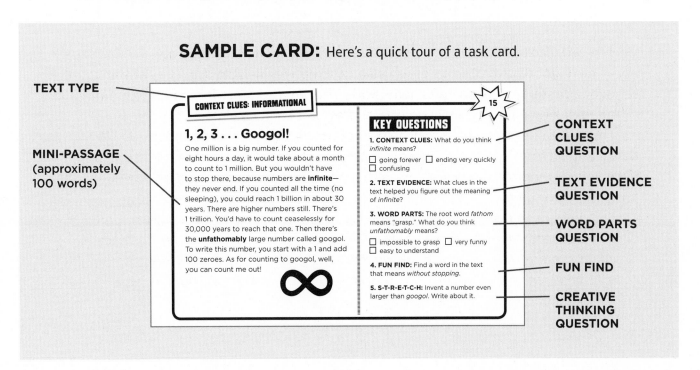

SAMPLE CARD: Here's a quick tour of a task card.

TEXT TYPE

MINI-PASSAGE (approximately 100 words)

CONTEXT CLUES QUESTION

TEXT EVIDENCE QUESTION

WORD PARTS QUESTION

FUN FIND

CREATIVE THINKING QUESTION

About the 12 Comprehension Helper Cards

To scaffold student learning, we've provided 12 Comprehension Helper cards. (See pages 10–15.) These "bonus" cards, related to context clues and key comprehension topics, are intended to provide age-perfect background information that will help students respond knowledgeably to the five questions on the 100 task cards. We suggest you photocopy a set for each student to have at the ready.

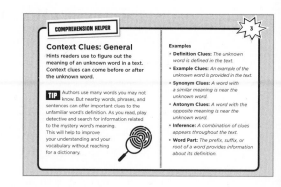

About the Answer Key

We've also included a complete answer key. (See pages 67–78.) In the key, we've provided sample responses to the questions on all 100 cards. Please note that student answers will vary. Because many of the questions are open-ended and no two minds work exactly alike, we encourage you to accept all reasonable answers.

MAKING THE TASK CARDS

The task cards are easy to make. Just photocopy the pages and cut along the dashed lines.

- **Tip #1:** For sturdier cards, photocopy the pages onto card stock and/or laminate them.

- **Tip #2:** To make the cards extra appealing, use different colors of paper or card stock for each category.

- **Tip #3:** To store the cards, use a plastic lunch bag or a recipe box. Or, hole-punch the corner of each card and place cards on a key ring.

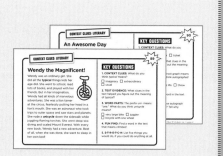

First-Time Teaching Routine With the Cards

Any text will become accessible to students who bring strong reading strategies to the table. Here's an easy routine for introducing the task cards to your students for the very first time.

1. Discuss how to use context clues to determine the meaning of unfamiliar words in nonfiction and fiction.

2. Introduce or review the six main types of context clues: definitions, examples, synonyms, antonyms, inferences, and word parts. **TIP:** Share some or all of the Comprehension Helper cards on pages 10–15.

3. Display an enlarged version of the task card using an interactive whiteboard, document camera, or overhead projector.

4. Cover the mini-passage and display just the title. Read it aloud and invite students to predict what the nonfiction or fiction story will be about.

5. Read the mini-passage aloud, slowly and clearly.

6. Boost fluency by inviting a student volunteer to read the mini-passage again using his or her best performance voice.

7. Discuss the mini-passage. Encourage students to comment and connect it to other articles and books they've read, as well as to their own lives.

8. Prepare to number and record each answer on a chart pad. Explain to students that they will be using complete sentences with proper spelling and punctuation to answer each question.

9. Discuss question one, **Context Clues**. Show children how to "mine" the text that comes right before and after the bold vocabulary word to help determine its definition. Use a highlighter to underline key words and phrases related to the word's meaning. Ask kids to tell you which type of clue or clues they located: definition, example, synonym, antonym, inference, or word part. Demonstrate how to answer the questions in a complete sentence using this writing frame: _Word means "definition of word."_ Example: _Infinite means "to go on and on forever."_

10. Discuss question two, **Text Evidence**. Demonstrate how to respond in a full sentence using this writing frame: _The passage says, "supporting text from passage."_ Example: _The passage says, "Because numbers are infinite, they never end."_

11. Discuss question three, **Word Parts**. Explain how to use the featured word part to unlock the meaning of the word. Ask: _Is it a prefix or suffix?_ If possible, make a list of other words that contain the same root. How are their meanings similar? Demonstrate how to answer the questions in a complete sentence using this writing frame: _Word means "definition of word."_ Example: _Incomprehensibly means "impossible to understand."_

12. Discuss question four, **Fun Find**. Invite a student to find the mystery word and underline key words and phrases that helped to determine its meaning. Demonstrate how to answer the questions in a complete sentence using this writing frame: *Mystery word means "definition of word."* Example: *Ceaselessly means "without stopping."*

13. Discuss question five, **S-T-R-E-T-C-H**. Work together to respond to the question in a meaningful way.

14. Give your class a round of applause for successfully completing a task card. Now they're ready to tackle the cards independently.

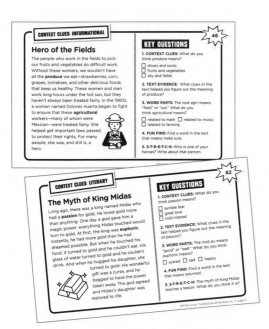

10 WAYS TO USE THE TASK CARDS

The task cards can be used in many ways. Here are 10 quick ideas to maximize learning.

- Challenge students to complete one task card every morning.

- Invite partners to read the task cards together and respond in writing.

- Ask small groups to read, discuss, and respond to the task cards orally.

- Place the task cards in a learning center for students to complete independently.

- Carve out time to do a task card with the whole class a few times a week.

- Encourage individual students to build fluency by reading a task card aloud to the class. They can then solicit answers from fellow students.

- Laminate the task cards and place them in a recipe box for students to do after they've completed the rest of their work.

- Send the task cards home for students to complete, with or without parental help.

- Provide students with designated notebooks for recording the answers to all of the task cards.

- Create a class chart, telling students to make a check mark each time they complete a task card. The first student to reach 100 wins a prize!

CONNECTION TO THE STANDARDS

The lessons in this book support the College and Career Readiness Anchor Standards for Reading for students in grades K–12. These broad standards, which serve as the basis for many state standards, were developed to establish rigorous educational expectations with the goal of providing students nationwide with a quality education that prepares them for college and careers. The chart below details how the lessons align with specific reading standards for informational and literary texts for students in grades 4 through 6.

These materials also address language standards, including skills in the conventions of standard English, knowledge of language, and vocabulary acquisition and use. In addition, students who write out their responses meet writing standards as they answer the questions about each mini-passage and demonstrate their ability to convey ideas about the text clearly and coherently.

INFORMATIONAL TEXT

Key Ideas and Details

- Refer to details and examples in a text when explaining what the text says explicitly and when drawing inferences from the text.
- Quote accurately from a text when explaining what the text says explicitly and when drawing inferences from the text.
- Cite textual evidence to support analysis of what the text says explicitly as well as inferences drawn from the text.

Craft and Structure

- Determine the meaning of general academic and domain-specific words or phrases in a text relevant to an age-appropriate topic or subject area.
- Describe the overall structure (e.g., chronology, comparison, cause–effect, problem–solution) of events, ideas, concepts, or information in a text or part of a text.

Integration of Knowledge and Ideas

- Explain how an author uses reasons and evidence to support particular points in a text.
- Analyze how a particular sentence, paragraph, chapter, or section fits into the overall structure of a text and contributes to the development of the ideas.
- Trace and evaluate the argument and specific claims in a text, distinguishing claims that are supported by reasons and evidence from claims that are not.

LITERARY TEXT

Key Ideas and Details

- Refer to details and examples in a text when explaining what the text says explicitly and when drawing inferences from the text.
- Determine a theme of a story, drama, or poem from details in the text; summarize the text.
- Describe in depth a character, setting, or event in a story or drama, drawing on specific details in the text (e.g., a character's thoughts, words, or actions).
- Quote accurately from a text when explaining what the text says explicitly and when drawing inferences from the text.
- Cite textual evidence to support analysis of what the text says explicitly as well as inferences drawn from the text.
- Describe how a particular story or drama unfolds in a series of episodes, as well as how the characters respond or change as the plot moves toward a resolution.

Craft and Structure

- Determine the meaning of words and phrases as they are used in a text, including those that allude to significant characters found in mythology (e.g., *Herculean*, referring to Hercules).
- Compare and contrast two or more characters, settings, or events in a story or drama, drawing on specific details in the text (e.g., how characters interact).
- Analyze how a particular sentence, chapter, scene, or stanza fits into the overall structure of a text and contributes to the development of the theme, setting, or plot.

Informational Text

Text that provides facts and information to readers.

TIP *Before reading*, think about what you already know about the topic. Also think about questions you'd like answered in the text. *During reading*, take your time. Try to determine the main idea and key details. Reread any confusing parts. *After reading*, reflect on what you just read. Talk about the text with a classmate.

Examples

- *news stories*
- *textbooks*
- *business memos*
- *magazine articles*
- *advertisements*
- *personal essays*
- *humor essays*
- *nonfiction books*
- *health-care pamphlets*
- *assembly instructions*
- *campaign information*

- *biographies*
- *sports articles*
- *history texts*
- *editorials*
- *recipes*
- *opinion pieces*
- *memoirs*

Literary Text

A piece of writing, such as a story or poem, that has the purpose of telling a tale or entertaining.

TIP *Before reading*, look at the title. What do you think the story will be about? *During reading*, stop and make predictions about what will happen next. Reread the parts you especially like or find confusing. *After reading*, reflect on the story. Compare it to other books and even movies, as well as your own life. Ask yourself, "What did the author want to tell me? What did I learn?"

Examples

- *fantasy*
- *science fiction*
- *thrillers*
- *legends*
- *folktales*
- *tall tales*
- *horror*
- *romance*
- *tragedy*
- *adventure*
- *friendship*

- *realistic fiction*
- *mysteries*
- *comedies*
- *fairy tales*
- *fables*
- *drama*
- *poems*
- *short stories*
- *plays*

COMPREHENSION HELPER

Context Clues: General

Hints readers use to figure out the meaning of an unknown word in a text. Context clues can come before or after the unknown word.

TIP Authors use many words you may not know. But nearby words, phrases, and sentences can offer important clues to the unfamiliar word's definition. As you read, play detective and search for information related to the mystery word's meaning. This will help to improve your understanding and your vocabulary without reaching for a dictionary.

Examples

- **Definition Clues:** *The unknown word is defined in the text.*
- **Example Clues:** *An example of the unknown word is provided in the text.*
- **Synonym Clues:** *A word with a similar meaning is near the unknown word.*
- **Antonym Clues:** *A word with the opposite meaning is near the unknown word.*
- **Inference:** *A combination of clues appears throughout the text.*
- **Word Part:** *The prefix, suffix, or root of a word provides information about its definition.*

COMPREHENSION HELPER

Context Clues: Definition

A DEFINITION is when the meaning of an unknown word appears near that word in the text.

TIP If you encounter an unknown word, don't reach for the dictionary without first rereading the "neighborhood text" surrounding it. Sometimes you will even encounter that word's actual definition! That definition can appear before or after the mystery word. (See examples at right, with unknown words in *bold*.)

Examples

- *Anna was <u>always happy and full of energy</u>. She was a very **ebullient** girl!*
- ***Owlets** is the name for <u>baby owls</u>.*
- *My cousin is a very **gregarious** kid. He <u>loves the company of others</u>.*
- *Hawaii is <u>a chain of islands</u>. That makes it an **archipelago**.*
- *Some immigrant women worked as **seamstresses**, <u>supporting themselves by sewing</u>.*
- *The <u>very large</u> gem was actually a **humongous** diamond!*

Context Clues: Synonym

A SYNONYM is a word that means almost the same thing as the unknown word.

TIP A synonym is very similar to a definition except a synonym is just a single word. If you encounter a mystery word, be on the lookout for a nearby synonym to help you unlock the unknown word's meaning. (See examples at right, with unknown words in *bold*.)

Examples

- *Jonathan is **lanky**. He's quite <u>tall</u>, and very good at basketball.*
- *The <u>lonely</u> island feels very **desolate** today.*
- *Lesha is totally **hilarious**. That girl is so <u>funny</u>!*
- *The sun was <u>hidden</u> because it was **obscured** by clouds.*
- *My grandad loves to take <u>walks</u>. He calls them his **constitutionals**.*
- *We named my cat <u>Lazy</u> because she is very **lethargic**.*

Context Clues: Antonym

An ANTONYM is the opposite of the unknown word. That makes it the opposite of a synonym, too.

TIP Sometimes authors provide context for an unknown word by including its antonym in the text. When you encounter a word you don't know, play detective and be on the lookout for a word that might actually have the opposite meaning! (See examples at right, with unknown words in *bold*.)

Examples

- *Jada is not **diminutive**. In fact, she is actually quite <u>tall</u>!*
- *Most of Kentucky is not <u>urban</u>. It is **rural**.*
- *The adult is called an <u>alpaca</u>, while its baby is called a **cria**.*
- *Josef is always <u>cheerful</u>. The kid is never **irascible**.*
- *The rain forest is **lush**, as opposed to <u>barren</u>.*
- *No one would accuse the **rowdy** soccer players of being too <u>quiet</u>.*

COMPREHENSION HELPER

Context Clues: Example

An EXAMPLE illustrates the meaning of an unknown word. Sometimes the context clue is one example and sometimes it is several examples.

TIP When you encounter an example or examples in a text, stop! They could well be context clues to help you arrive at the meaning of a mystery word. (See examples at right, with unknown words in *bold*.)

Examples

- *Rabbits, cats, horses, and people are all **mammals**.*
- *A clarinet is a type of **woodwind** instrument.*
- *Healthy forms of **locomotion** are walking, running, and biking.*
- *They chattered on the bus and at school, too. One could say they were **loquacious**.*
- *A caterpillar becoming a butterfly is a good example of **metamorphosis**.*
- *Beethoven, Bach, and the Beatles were all **virtuoso** musicians.*
- *Roses and daisies, which bloom every year, are two kinds of **perennial** flowers.*

COMPREHENSION HELPER

Context Clues: Inferences

INFERENCES are clues scattered throughout the text that help you arrive at an unknown word's definition. Inferences are like puzzle pieces that each contribute to the understanding of a mystery word.

TIP Inferences are hard to define. These random clues can be partial definitions, semi-examples, or mood-related words. They may help you without your even knowing it! For that reason, it's often a good idea to read a passage more than once. (See examples at right, with unknown words in *bold*.)

Examples

- *Ghosts hid in the spooky trees. There was an **eerie** feel in the odd, autumn air.*
- *Independent Louisa was a real **autodidact**. She loved learning and read everything in sight.*
- *It was February and the cold wind was very **blustery**.*
- *Worried Jason was **perturbed** to learn that he failed the math test.*
- *Maria **chortled** loudly at the funny joke.*
- *Leo's writing was as **luminous** as a bright, sunny day!*

Context Clues: Word Parts

Knowing the meaning of word parts such as *dis, pre, able*, and *ful* can help you figure out the definition of unknown words such as *disregard, preview, agreeable*, and *youthful.* These "roots" are very old and often come from classic Greek and Latin languages.

TIP Roots that come at the beginning of a word are called *prefixes*. The Greek root *geo* means "world" and can be found in the words *geography* and *geophysics*. Roots that come at the end of words are called *suffixes*. The Latin root *tain* means "hold" and can be found in the words *abstain* and *obtain*.

Examples

PREFIXES

- The Greek root *dis* means "not." You can find it in: *dislike, disregard, disappear, disloyal,* and *dismount.*

- The Latin root *pre* means "before." You can find it in: *prearrange, precook, preschool, prepay, and prevail.*

SUFFIXES

- The Greek root *able* means "having the power." You can find it in: *agreeable, excusable, fashionable, and wearable.*

- The Latin root *ful* means "filled with." You can find it in: *artful, distasteful, bountiful, gleeful,* and *resourceful.*

Text Evidence

Words, phrases, or sentences in a text that provide information, answer a question, or help you understand the meaning of an unknown word.

TIP When you come across a word you don't know, be on the lookout for text evidence to help you figure out its meaning. These clues in the passages can take the form of a definition, a synonym, an antonym, an example, an inference, or a word part. (Sometimes there can be more than one of them!) Always use a full sentence when providing text evidence as shown on the right.

Examples

*Tom the Troll was very cranky indeed. He always argued and seldom said a kind word to anyone. "Why are you so **cantankerous**?" asked Billy Goat Bob.*

Question 1, Context Clues: What do you think *cantankerous* means?

Answer: *Cantankerous* means "bad-tempered."

Question 2, Text Evidence: What clues helped you figure out the meaning of *cantankerous?*

Answer: The passage says, *"Tom the Troll was very cranky indeed. He always argued and seldom said a kind word to anyone."*

Summarize

To create a brief statement about a text using only the most important details.

TIP When writing a summary, think about how to retell the key ideas of a passage in your own words. Challenge yourself to be short and clear *and* to leave out all the unimportant details.

Example

- **Sample Text:** *Cats make excellent pets. From Nepal to New York— cats are the world's favorite pet! Cats are mammals, like bears and bats. The difference is that cats are gentle and enjoy living with people. There are more than 70 breeds of cats. Cats are fairly easy to care for. Unlike dogs, they don't need to be walked several times a day. Plus, they love to sleep. In fact, some cats sleep up to 20 hours a day.*

- **Summary of Text:** *Cats make excellent pets for people all over the world. There are more than 70 different breeds of this gentle mammal. Cats are easy to care for.*

Prediction

To use what you know from the text to make a smart guess about what will happen later on in the story.

TIP When you read a story, pause and play detective. Collect clues in the text and use them to make smart guesses about what will happen next. Making predictions keeps you actively engaged with the text and improves your comprehension.

Examples

- *I know that the castle is haunted, so I **predict** the main character will see a ghost.*

- *I know the wolf blew down the straw house, so I **predict** he will blow down the stick house, too.*

- *I know the main character is lonely, so I **predict** she will try to find a friend.*

- *I know the frog was once a prince, so I **predict** he will turn into a prince again.*

- *I know the story takes place in a circus, so I **predict** it will include clowns and animals.*

100
CONTEXT CLUES
TASK CARDS

CONTEXT CLUES: INFORMATIONAL

All About Bats

Bats are fantastic! They can fly like birds. However, they are not birds. That's partly because they are covered with fur rather than feathers. They are mammals, the same as pandas, pigs, and people. Bats are **nocturnal**. They sleep during the day, hanging upside down. When the sun sets, they emerge from barns and caves. They are very busy at night. They fly around hunting for food. Bats are **omnivores**. They eat small creatures such as insects, frogs, and fish. They also enjoy fruits such as mangoes and bananas. Bats are fantastic!

KEY QUESTIONS

1. CONTEXT CLUES: What do you think *nocturnal* means?

☐ active during the day ☐ very sleepy
☐ active at night

2. TEXT EVIDENCE: What clues in the text helped you figure out the meaning of *nocturnal*?

3. WORD PARTS: The prefix *omni-* means "all." What do you think *omnivores* means?

☐ animals that eat at night
☐ animals that eat plants and animals
☐ animals that eat only plants

4. FUN FIND: Find a word in the text that means *to come out of*.

5. S-T-R-E-T-C-H: Are you an *omnivore*? Tell why or why not.

CONTEXT CLUES: INFORMATIONAL

2

Hungry Dads!

How long can you go without eating? After a few hours, your stomach probably rumbles and you're ready for a snack. Imagine **abstaining from** food for two whole months! That's how long male emperor penguins go without eating. After the female lays her egg, she takes off for two months and fishes for food. The male stays behind and guards the egg. He keeps it warm and secure by holding it on his feet, covered by a fold of skin. When the mom returns, the dad is **liberated** from his duties. Finally, it's his turn to eat. He heads to the ocean to fish for food.

KEY QUESTIONS

1. CONTEXT CLUES: What do you think *abstaining from* means?

☐ going without ☐ eating
☐ forgetting

2. TEXT EVIDENCE: What clues in the text helped you figure out the meaning of *abstaining from*?

3. WORD PARTS: The root *liber* means "free." What do you think *liberated* means?

☐ committed ☐ released ☐ angered

4. FUN FIND: Find a word in the text that means *safe*.

5. S-T-R-E-T-C-H: Write a paragraph on a topic of your choice. Include the words *abstain* and *liberate*.

CONTEXT CLUES: INFORMATIONAL

What's in a Name?

When you were little, did you read *The Cat in the Hat*? How about *Green Eggs and Ham* or *Horton Hears a Who*? All of these books were written  by the popular children's author Dr. Seuss. Dr. Seuss is one of the most **acclaimed** children's writers of all time. People the world over applaud and praise his funny stories. But did you know this well-loved author wasn't really a doctor? In reality, "Dr. Seuss" was not his real name but a **pseudonym** that he used for his books. His actual name was Theodor Geisel. Dr. Seuss's fun books are filled with rhymes that make them pleasurable to read at any age. Pick one up and see what you think!

KEY QUESTIONS

1. CONTEXT CLUES: What do you think *acclaimed* means?

☐ silly ☐ forgotten
☐ well known and loved

2. TEXT EVIDENCE: What clues in the text helped you figure out the meaning of *acclaimed*?

3. WORD PARTS: The prefix *pseudo-* means *false*. What do you think *pseudonym* means?

☐ pretend name
☐ doctor's name
☐ famous author

4. FUN FIND: Find a second word in the text that means *enjoyable*.

5. S-T-R-E-T-C-H: If you had a *pseudonym,* what would it be? Why?

CONTEXT CLUES: INFORMATIONAL

The Curse of Spring

Every year when spring arrives, many people feel **elated**. They are happy that the weather is warmer, the snow has melted, and the flowers are in bloom. But not everyone is thrilled about spring. For some, spring means allergies! When the flowers and trees burst into bloom, they release pollen that causes certain people to have allergic **rhinitis**. For them, the vivid blossoms of spring can mean lots of nose blowing and difficulty breathing. Fortunately,  there are ways to treat these seasonal allergies, so even allergy sufferers can enjoy the flowers.

KEY QUESTIONS

1. CONTEXT CLUES: What do you think *elated* means?

☐ tired ☐ happy ☐ afraid

2. TEXT EVIDENCE: What clues in the text helped you figure out the meaning of *elated*?

3. WORD PARTS: The root *rhini* means "nose." What do you think *rhinitis* means?

☐ itchy eye
☐ irritated nose
☐ irritated rhino

4. FUN FIND: Find a word in the text that means *colorful and bright*.

5. S-T-R-E-T-C-H: What's something that makes you *elated*? Write about it.

Our Planets

There are eight planets in our solar system. In addition to Earth, there's Mercury, Venus, Mars, Jupiter, Saturn, Uranus, and Neptune. These eight planets all **rotate** around our sun. For a long time, there was a ninth planet, Pluto. In 2006, a group of scientists decided that Pluto wasn't actually a planet after all. They said it was too small to be a "real" planet. They **demoted** Pluto, saying it was only a "dwarf planet." Not everyone was content with this decision, but the official count is now eight planets in our solar system.

KEY QUESTIONS

1. CONTEXT CLUES: What do you think *rotate* means?

☐ shoot lasers at
☐ stand by
☐ move around

2. TEXT EVIDENCE: What clues in the text helped you figure out the meaning of *rotate*?

3. WORD PARTS: The root *mote* means "move." What do you think *demoted* means?

☐ named ☐ visited ☐ lowered

4. FUN FIND: Find a word in the text that means *happy*.

5. S-T-R-E-T-C-H: What is your favorite planet? Tell why.

Mosquitoes in the Rain

What do mosquitoes do in a rainstorm? They're such **diminutive** creatures. A single raindrop can be 50 times their size! But guess what? Even in a downpour, these insects fly anyway. For tiny mosquitoes, the drops seem far apart. Most of the time, they're able to **evade** the falling rain, flying between the drops. When one gets hit, the mosquito simply goes with the drop. It plummets toward the earth, weighted down by the water drop. Almost always, the mosquito is able to break free before the drop hits the ground. Besides being annoying pests, mosquitoes are also great escape artists.

KEY QUESTIONS

1. CONTEXT CLUES: What do you think *diminutive* means?

☐ very small ☐ very annoying
☐ very large

2. TEXT EVIDENCE: What clues in the text helped you figure out the meaning of *diminutive*?

3. WORD PARTS: The prefix *e-* can mean "away." What do you think *evade* means?

☐ enjoy ☐ invade ☐ get away from

4. FUN FIND: Find a word in the text that means *fall quickly*.

5. S-T-R-E-T-C-H: Imagine you're a mosquito. Turn on your imagination and describe your flight through a rainstorm.

CONTEXT CLUES: INFORMATIONAL

Ahoy or Hello?

The owners of the first telephones weren't sure what **greeting** to use. They didn't know what to say to start a conversation. Alexander Graham Bell, who invented the telephone in 1876, strongly believed people should say, "ahoy." That was a word used on ships. Thomas Edison was convinced that "hello" was **preferable**. Back then, *hello* was a fairly new word, less than 100 years old. The matter was settled by the instructions printed in the first phone books. Callers were told to answer with "hello." To end a call, they should say, "That is all." Aren't you glad "that is all" didn't catch on? Doesn't it sound kind of rude?

KEY QUESTIONS

1. CONTEXT CLUES: What do you think *greeting* means?

☐ word of anger ☐ word of welcome
☐ mouthpiece

2. TEXT EVIDENCE: What clues in the text helped you figure out the meaning of *greeting*?

3. WORD PARTS: The suffix *-able* can mean "to be." What do you think *preferable* means?

☐ to be worse ☐ to be better
☐ to be louder

4. FUN FIND: Find a word in the text that means *to be sure of something*.

5. S-T-R-E-T-C-H: Invent some words or phrases to use instead of *hello* and *goodbye*.

CONTEXT CLUES: INFORMATIONAL

No Ropes

Maybe you've climbed over big rocks or **boulders** while on a hike. Maybe you've even gone to a climbing wall and used ropes to help you **ascend** it. But expert rock climbers scale super-steep mountains, and some of them do it with no ropes at all! Climbing without ropes is known as "free soloing," and it takes a lot of expertise and many years of practice. In 2017, climber Alex Honnold free-soloed to the top of

El Capitan, an incredibly steep mountain in Yosemite National Park that is *very* hard to climb, even with ropes! He's the only person in the world who's ever done it.

KEY QUESTIONS

1. CONTEXT CLUES: What do you think *boulders* means?

☐ large rocks ☐ rivers ☐ waterfalls

2. TEXT EVIDENCE: What clues in the text helped you figure out the meaning of *boulders*?

3. WORD PARTS: The root *scend* means "go." What do you think *ascend* means?

☐ climb up ☐ fall down ☐ jump over

4. FUN FIND: Find a word in the text that means *skill*.

5. S-T-R-E-T-C-H: Would you like to learn how to go mountain climbing? Why or why not?

CONTEXT CLUES: INFORMATIONAL

Bubblegum Inventor

Have you heard of Walter Diemer? He's the man who invented bubblegum. In 1928, Diemer worked at a company that made chewing gum. In his spare time, Diemer experimented with new kinds of gum. His goal was to create gum that could **expand**. It needed to blow up like a balloon, getting bigger and bigger. After an entire year of work, Diemer figured it out. But then he lost his formula for making bubblegum! It took him four months to **reinvent** it. As one final step, Diemer decided to color his new gum pink. Next time you blow a big bubble, remember to thank Walter Diemer.

KEY QUESTIONS

1. CONTEXT CLUES: What do you think *expand* means?

☐ become smaller ☐ lose its flavor
☐ become larger

2. TEXT EVIDENCE: What clues in the text helped you figure out the meaning of *expand*?

3. WORD PARTS: The prefix *re-* means "again." What do you think *reinvent* means?

☐ lose again ☐ tell someone about
☐ invent again

4. FUN FIND: Find a word in the text that means a *list of ingredients*.

5. S-T-R-E-T-C-H: Write a note to Walter Diemer to say thank you for inventing bubblegum.

CONTEXT CLUES: INFORMATIONAL

Amazing Hummingbirds

Have you ever seen a hummingbird? These tiny birds are often no more than three or four inches long. Their small wings flutter so fast that they can **hover** in the air, staying in the same spot, as if they're treading water in midair. They can also fly backwards and even upside down! Just how fast do their wings go? Some species of hummingbirds can flap their wings a **maximum** of 200 times a second! All that rapid flapping creates a soft humming sound. As you may have guessed, that's how hummingbirds got their name.

KEY QUESTIONS

1. CONTEXT CLUES: What do you think *hover* means?

☐ fly in the same place ☐ fly quickly
☐ fly upside down

2. TEXT EVIDENCE: What clues in the text helped you figure out the meaning of *hover*?

3. WORD PARTS: The root *max* means "greatest." What do you think *maximum* means?

☐ least amount ☐ normal amount
☐ most amount

4. FUN FIND: Find a word in the text that means *fast*.

5. S-T-R-E-T-C-H: Write a paragraph about another animal that you think is amazing, and tell why.

Pyramids Are Everywhere

When you think of pyramids, you probably think of Egypt. But a pyramid is simply a **structure** with triangular sides. Throughout history, people have built pyramids in many different places. Ancient people in Greece and Sudan built pyramids. Central America is home to the largest number of pyramids. Mayans and Aztecs built them. Many of them still exist today in countries such as Mexico. Because it's a **beloved** shape, the pyramid is ubiquitous. There are even modern buildings that take this shape. For example, there's a hotel in Las Vegas that's a pyramid. There's also a tall, skinny pyramid skyscraper in San Francisco.

KEY QUESTIONS

1. CONTEXT CLUES: What do you think *structure* means?

☐ machine ☐ boat ☐ building

2. TEXT EVIDENCE: What clues in the text helped you figure out the meaning of *structure*?

3. WORD PARTS: The prefix *be-* can mean "very much." What do you think *beloved* means?

☐ very boring
☐ very hated
☐ very loved

4. FUN FIND: Find a word in the text that means *everywhere*.

5. S-T-R-E-T-C-H: Write a summary of this passage.

World Cup Winners

In 2019, the mighty U.S. women's soccer team won the World Cup. It defeated the Netherlands, 2–0. The U.S. team had been **dominant**, winning four out of the first eight World Cup tournaments. The U.S. won the very first one, back in 1991. It also managed two consecutive wins, in 2015 and 2019. The only other countries that have won are Germany, Norway, and Japan. During the 2019 tournament, the **undisputed** star of the U.S. team was Megan Rapinoe. She scored six goals. The women's soccer World Cup is held every four years. Who do you think will win the next one?

KEY QUESTIONS

1. CONTEXT CLUES: What do you think *dominant* means?

☐ most happy ☐ most powerful
☐ most tired

2. TEXT EVIDENCE: What clues in the text helped you figure out the meaning of *dominant*?

3. WORD PARTS: The prefix *un-* means "not." What do you think *undisputed* means?

☐ not challenged ☐ always incorrect
☐ very bad

4. FUN FIND: Find a word in the text that means *back-to-back*.

5. S-T-R-E-T-C-H: Write a sports story about a *dominant* team.

Sensational Sea Otters

Sea otters are the smallest of the ocean mammals. They don't **reside** in deep, warm water. Instead, they live in shallow, icy waters, such as the northern Pacific Ocean. Sea otters have lots of fur to keep them warm. In fact, their fur consists of two layers, an underlayer and an overlayer. Air gets trapped between the two layers, which creates a cushion to keep otters toasty in the chilliest waters. They also eat a lot to stay warm, **ingesting** up to 30 percent of their weight in food every day. That means if a sea otter weighs 90 pounds, it eats up to 27 pounds of fish in one day!

KEY QUESTIONS

1. CONTEXT CLUES: What do you think *reside* means?

☐ love ☐ live ☐ sleep

2. TEXT EVIDENCE: What clues in the text helped you figure out the meaning of *reside*?

3. WORD PARTS: The root *gest* means "carry." What do you think *ingesting* means?

☐ taking in ☐ throwing away ☐ losing

4. FUN FIND: Find a word in the text that means *not very deep*.

5. S-T-R-E-T-C-H: What are some ways to stay warm if you don't have toasty fur like a sea otter? Make a list.

Life-Saving Mold!

When you think of mold, you probably think: *Yuck!* You might **visualize** images of food gone bad. You picture slimy, green fungus growing on bread or a piece of fruit. Sometimes mold *is* pretty gross. But some molds are more friend than foe, and one in particular is life-saving! That mold is called penicillin. In the year 1928, a scientist named Alexander Fleming discovered that the penicillin mold killed harmful germs and bacteria. Today, people everywhere take the **antibiotic** known as penicillin when they have an infection such as strep throat. This mold truly is a winner!

KEY QUESTIONS

1. CONTEXT CLUES: What do you think *visualize* means?

☐ delete ☐ picture in your mind ☐ draw

2. TEXT EVIDENCE: What clues in the text helped you figure out the meaning of *visualize*?

3. WORD PARTS: The prefix *anti-* means "against." What do you think *antibiotic* means?

☐ medicine that kills germs ☐ spoiled food ☐ medicine that helps germs grow

4. FUN FIND: Find a word in the text that means *enemy*.

5. S-T-R-E-T-C-H: Can you think of more words that include the prefix *anti-*? Make a list.

1, 2, 3 . . . Googol!

One million is a big number. If you counted for eight hours a day, it would take about a month to count to 1 million. But you wouldn't have to stop there, because numbers are **infinite**—they never end. If you counted all the time (no sleeping), you could reach 1 billion in about 30 years. There are higher numbers still. There's 1 trillion. You'd have to count ceaselessly for 30,000 years to reach that one. Then there's the **unfathomably** large number called googol. To write this number, you start with a 1 and add 100 zeroes. As for counting to googol, well, you can count me out!

KEY QUESTIONS

1. CONTEXT CLUES: What do you think *infinite* means?

☐ going forever   ☐ ending very quickly
☐ confusing

2. TEXT EVIDENCE: What clues in the text helped you figure out the meaning of *infinite*?

3. WORD PARTS: The root word *fathom* means "grasp." What do you think *unfathomably* means?

☐ impossible to grasp   ☐ very funny
☐ easy to understand

4. FUN FIND: Find a word in the text that means *without stopping*.

5. S-T-R-E-T-C-H: Invent a number even larger than *googol*. Write about it.

Madame Doctor

Today, if you go to the doctor, the person you see might be a man or a woman. For a long time, being a doctor wasn't thought of as a proper **occupation** for women. Women were expected to work in jobs like teachers, nannies, or cooks. If they wanted to work in medicine, women were only allowed to be nurses, and they were **excluded from** medical schools. In 1848, Elizabeth Blackwell became the first woman to earn a medical degree. Even after Blackwell, it was a while before women were welcomed as doctors. Today, even more women than men go to medical school and become physicians. How times have changed!

KEY QUESTIONS

1. CONTEXT CLUES: What do you think *occupation* means?

☐ medicine   ☐ job   ☐ game

2. TEXT EVIDENCE: What clues in the text helped you figure out the meaning of *occupation*?

3. WORD PARTS: The prefix *ex-* means "out." What do you think *excluded from* means?

☐ kicked out of   ☐ not let in
☐ studied hard

4. FUN FIND: Find a word in the text that means *doctors*.

5. S-T-R-E-T-C-H: It takes many years of school to become a doctor. Is that a good thing? Why do you think so?

Good Enough to Eat?

When it comes to the pictures of food in magazines and on TV, looks can be **deceiving**. What you see in photos isn't always real. Food photographers use lots of tricks to make food look like the height of **gastronomy**. But even food that looks delicious might not be. That syrup on the pancakes? It just might be motor oil. Unlike genuine syrup, motor oil won't soak into the pancakes. How about that milk in the cereal bowl? It might actually be glue! Milk makes cereal soggy, but flakes stay crispy in a bowl full of glue. So remember, what you see isn't always what you get!

KEY QUESTIONS

1. CONTEXT CLUES: What do you think *deceiving* means?

☐ real ☐ delicious ☐ untrue

2. TEXT EVIDENCE: What clues in the text helped you figure out the meaning of *deceiving*?

3. WORD PARTS: The root *gastro* means "stomach." What do you think *gastronomy* means?

☐ good cooking ☐ motor oil
☐ a starry sky

4. FUN FIND: Find a word in the text that means *real*.

5. S-T-R-E-T-C-H: A *gastronome* is someone who loves good food. Who is the best cook you know? What is his or her specialty?

It All Started With *Bertie the Brain*

The first video game was created in 1950. It was called *Bertie the Brain*, and it was very **elementary**—just a simple game of tic-tac-toe. Yet, one needed a 12-foot-tall computer to play it. Then, in 1969, the game *Space Travel* was created. The goal was to land a ship on a planet. These early games were played mostly by scientists and professors. After all, one needed an **enormous** computer to play. The breakthrough came in 1972 with *Pong*. *Pong* was simply video Ping-Pong. But it could run on a television set. Because many people owned TVs, *Pong* became a huge hit. Soon video games became super popular.

KEY QUESTIONS

1. CONTEXT CLUES: What do you think *elementary* means?

☐ hard ☐ easy ☐ expensive

2. TEXT EVIDENCE: What clues in the text helped you figure out the meaning of *elementary*?

3. WORD PARTS: The root *norm* means "normal." What do you think *enormous* means?

☐ smaller than normal
☐ perfectly normal
☐ larger than normal

4. FUN FIND: Find a word in the text that means *important change*.

5. S-T-R-E-T-C-H: Are video games good, bad, or in between? Write about it.

CONTEXT CLUES: INFORMATIONAL

Are You Superstitious?

Some people are **skittish** of black cats. Others are afraid to walk under ladders. Still others avoid the number 13 and won't open an umbrella indoors. All of these are examples of superstitions. People who are superstitious often fear that something bad will occur if they do something specific. Some superstitions, though, are related to *good* luck, like the belief that if you cross your fingers, something **beneficial** will happen. There are people who are superstitious about just one or two things, but others have a whole long list of things to do or dodge. What about you? Are you superstitious?

KEY QUESTIONS

1. CONTEXT CLUES: What do you think *skittish* means?

☐ fearful ☐ lucky ☐ unlucky

2. TEXT EVIDENCE: What clues in the text helped you figure out the meaning of *skittish*?

3. WORD PARTS: The root *bene* means "good." What do you think *beneficial* means?

☐ involving bad luck
☐ favorable
☐ worrisome

4. FUN FIND: Find a word in the text that means *avoid*.

5. S-T-R-E-T-C-H: Can you think of other superstitions? Make a list.

CONTEXT CLUES: INFORMATIONAL

What Is the Moon?

What is the moon? It's neither a star nor a planet. Moons have their own special place in space. Moons **orbit** planets, going around and around them. Earth has a moon, but there are many moons besides ours. While Earth has a single moon, some planets have more than one. Mars has two moons. Neptune has at least 14. Some planets have myriad moons. Saturn has more than 50. Jupiter has 79 and maybe more. **Astronomers** are still discovering new moons circling distant planets.

KEY QUESTIONS

1. CONTEXT CLUES: What do you think *orbit* means?

☐ circle around ☐ bite ☐ crash into

2. TEXT EVIDENCE: What clues in the text helped you figure out the meaning of *orbit*?

3. WORD PARTS: The prefix *astro-* means "related to space." What do you think *astronomers* means?

☐ people who ride in spaceships
☐ scientists who study space
☐ space aliens

4. FUN FIND: Find a word in the text that means *a very large number of.*

5. S-T-R-E-T-C-H: Would you like to go to the moon? Write about it.

Arctic Giant

Polar bears are huge, snowy-white members of the bear family, which is technically known as *ursidae*. These **massive** creatures can weigh as much as 1,500 pounds. They maintain their large size with a **carnivorous** diet, feasting mainly on seals. They live in the Arctic Circle at the northernmost pole of Earth. But their numbers are shrinking. As the planet gets warmer, the sea ice is melting, and the bears' home is becoming endangered. The warmer temperatures also cause their food sources to decrease. Polar bears need our help to ensure they are protected for many years to come.

KEY QUESTIONS

1. CONTEXT CLUES: What do you think *massive* means?

☐ hungry ☐ small and light
☐ large and heavy

2. TEXT EVIDENCE: What clues in the text helped you figure out the meaning of *massive*?

3. WORD PARTS: The root *carne* means "meat." What do you think *carnivorous* means?

☐ plant-eating ☐ liquid
☐ meat-eating

4. FUN FIND: Find a word in the text that means *lessen*.

5. S-T-R-E-T-C-H: Can you make a list of some other animals in the *ursidae* family?

So Many Microbes!

The human body is made of cells. How many cells? A lot! The exact number varies from one person to the next, but experts say an **approximate** number is 37 trillion. That's the number 37 with 12 zeros after it: 37,000,000,000,000. But your body contains more than just cells. It's also home to lots of **microbes**, such as germs and bacteria. These infinitesimal creatures live on your skin and inside your body, especially in your digestive tract. Many of these microbes are friendly and keep you healthy! Just how many of these microbes are living on you? Experts say that we have roughly the same number of microbes as cells!

KEY QUESTIONS

1. CONTEXT CLUES: What do you think *approximate* means?

☐ completely wrong ☐ exact
☐ close but not exact

2. TEXT EVIDENCE: What clues in the text helped you figure out the meaning of *approximate*?

3. WORD PARTS: The root *micro* means "small." What do you think *microbes* means?

☐ microscopes ☐ small living things
☐ insects

4. FUN FIND: Find a word in the text that means *very tiny*.

5. S-T-R-E-T-C-H: Write a summary of this passage.

Why People Say "Pencil Lead"

What's a pencil tip made out of? Do you call it "lead"? Well, there's a story behind that. The ancient Romans had a very useful tool called a stylus. This **device** was a pointed rod, made of lead, which left behind a mark. In the 1500s, lead was replaced by graphite. Graphite is softer than lead and leaves a darker mark. At first, people wrote using a graphite rod wrapped in string. By the 1600s, people starting encasing the graphite in wood. The pencil was born! The ancient Roman stylus was the pencil's **forerunner**. To this day, people usually say "lead" instead of "graphite" when talking about pencils.

KEY QUESTIONS

1. CONTEXT CLUES: What do you think *device* means?

☐ outfit ☐ snack ☐ tool

2. TEXT EVIDENCE: What clues in the text helped you figure out the meaning of *device*?

3. WORD PARTS: The prefix *fore-* means "in front of." What do you think *forerunner* means?

☐ thing that came after
☐ thing for runners
☐ thing that came before

4. FUN FIND: Find a word in the text that means *covering and surrounding*.

5. S-T-R-E-T-C-H: Describe a device that you frequently use.

Big World, Small Countries

Our huge world has some very small countries. Monaco is **minuscule**, covering less than one square mile. The entire country is about the size of a very small town. Liechtenstein is nestled in the Alps, secreted away among tall mountain peaks. The country doesn't even have its own airport. To visit, you have to fly to nearby Switzerland. Tuvalu is an island nation located in the Pacific Ocean, near Australia. It is so distant from most places that it only gets a few thousand visitors **annually**. Which of these small countries would you like to visit?

KEY QUESTIONS

1. CONTEXT CLUES: What do you think *minuscule* means?

☐ large ☐ colorful ☐ tiny

2. TEXT EVIDENCE: What clues in the text helped you figure out the meaning of *minuscule*?

3. WORD PARTS: The root *ann* means "year." What do you think *annually* means?

☐ every holiday ☐ every year
☐ every day

4. FUN FIND: Find a word in the text that means *hidden*.

5. S-T-R-E-T-C-H: Would you rather live in a big or a small country? Write about it.

A New Name for Starfish

Have you ever seen a sea star? These incredible creatures used to be known as "starfish." But experts realized that name wasn't **accurate,** because these creatures aren't actually fish at all. They are a type of sea creature known as *echinoderms.* The experts decided a better name for starfish is "sea stars." There are lots of interesting facts about sea stars, but maybe the most fascinating one is that they can **regenerate** an arm if they happen to lose it. Growing back the lost limb can take many months, but that's okay. Sea stars live for about 35 years.

KEY QUESTIONS

1. CONTEXT CLUES: What do you think *accurate* means?

☐ correct ☐ short ☐ easy

2. TEXT EVIDENCE: What clues in the text helped you figure out the meaning of *accurate*?

3. WORD PARTS: The root *gen* means "make" or "produce." What do you think *regenerate* means?

☐ grow back ☐ swim away from
☐ cut off

4. FUN FIND: Find a word in the text that means *arm* or *leg*.

5. S-T-R-E-T-C-H: Write two sentences. In one, use the word *accurate*. In the other, use the word *regenerate.*

Who's #8?

Martin Van Buren is America's eighth president. He is often **overlooked**. Other presidents, such as George Washington and Abraham Lincoln, get more attention. But he's interesting nonetheless. Van Buren grew up in Old Kinderhook, New York. His primary language was Dutch. He spoke English as a second language. Van Buren dropped out of school at age 14. But he was a **tireless** worker and was elected president in 1836. His nickname  was OK, for his hometown, Old Kinderhook. Americans started saying "OK," and the term caught on. OK, now you know a bit about President Van Buren.

KEY QUESTIONS

1. CONTEXT CLUES: What do you think *overlooked* means?

☐ well remembered ☐ ignored
☐ shown as handsome

2. TEXT EVIDENCE: What clues in the text helped you figure out the meaning of *overlooked*?

3. WORD PARTS: The suffix *-less* means "without." What do you think *tireless* means?

☐ without losing energy ☐ frustrated
☐ sleepy

4. FUN FIND: Find a word in the text that means *first*.

5. S-T-R-E-T-C-H: Who is your favorite president? Why? Write a paragraph about that person.

CONTEXT CLUES: INFORMATIONAL

Not Only a Good Writer

J. K. Rowling is one of the most **accomplished** writers of all time. She's the author of the wildly popular Harry Potter series of books, which have been translated into 60 different languages. The series has sold more than 400 million copies. Because of her huge success, Rowling has earned a great deal of money. She has opted to give a lot of it to charities and organizations that are working to help people and make the world a better place. Not only is Rowling a great writer, but she is a true **humanitarian.**

KEY QUESTIONS

1. CONTEXT CLUES: What do you think *accomplished* means?

☐ successful ☐ happy ☐ wild

2. TEXT EVIDENCE: What clues in the text helped you figure out the meaning of *accomplished*?

3. WORD PARTS: The suffix *-arian* means "a person who." What do you think *humanitarian* means?

☐ wealthy person
☐ person who cares about people
☐ person who writes books

4. FUN FIND: Find a word in the text that means *chosen*.

5. S-T-R-E-T-C-H: If you became wealthy, what organizations would you give some of your money to? Why?

CONTEXT CLUES: INFORMATIONAL

A Horse Nap

Can you sleep standing up? If you were a horse, the answer would be yes. While horses do lie on the ground to sleep, they are also able to nap on their feet. The  benefit of sleeping while standing up is clear. If a **predator** comes along that wants to eat them, horses can run away quickly if they're already on their feet. It turns out that horses have the unusual capacity to rest one leg while the other three hold them up. They **alternate** which leg is resting, so each leg gets to take a break.

KEY QUESTIONS

1. CONTEXT CLUES: What do you think *predator* means?

☐ animal that eats other animals
☐ sleeping horse
☐ early human

2. TEXT EVIDENCE: What clues in the text helped you figure out the meaning of *predator*?

3. WORD PARTS: The root *alter* means "other." What do you think *alternate* means?

☐ relax ☐ change ☐ pause

4. FUN FIND: Find a word in the text that means *ability*.

5. S-T-R-E-T-C-H: Write a paragraph on animals now or in the past. Use the word *predator.*

Deserts, Hot and Cold

Deserts are more common than many people might imagine. In fact, one third of Earth is covered in desert. A desert is a place that gets very low **precipitation**, less than 10 inches of rain or snow per year. While deserts are dry, they aren't always hot. In fact, Antarctica is **classified as** a desert. That's because even though it's very cold, it gets little snow. Despite the harsh and challenging conditions, many animals can be found in the world's deserts. Africa's Sahara desert is home to camels and ostriches. Chilly Antarctica is home to penguins and seals.

KEY QUESTIONS

1. CONTEXT CLUES: What do you think *precipitation* means?

☐ windy weather ☐ rain and snow
☐ thunder and lightning

2. TEXT EVIDENCE: What clues in the text helped you figure out the meaning of *precipitation*?

3. WORD PARTS: The root *class* means "a group." What do you think *classified as* means?

☐ put together with ☐ late for
☐ kept separate from

4. FUN FIND: Find a word in the text that means *difficult* or *intense*.

5. S-T-R-E-T-C-H: What is your favorite type of weather? Write about it.

The 51st State?

Should Puerto Rico become America's 51st state? Some people think so. Puerto Rico is an island located about 1,000 miles south of Florida. It is a U.S. **territory**. That means it is part of the United States, but it does not have all the rights and benefits that the 50 states have. If Puerto Rico were given **statehood**, it would become equal to the other 50 states in all ways. That includes having representatives in Congress. Many Puerto Ricans support  making the island a state, but not everyone thinks it's a good idea. For now, the island remains a territory.

KEY QUESTIONS

1. CONTEXT CLUES: What do you think *territory* means?

☐ area of land ☐ forest ☐ island

2. TEXT EVIDENCE: What clues in the text helped you figure out the meaning of *territory*?

3. WORD PARTS: The suffix *-hood* means "being." What do you think *statehood* means?

☐ being a state
☐ being near Florida
☐ being far away

4. FUN FIND: Find a word in the text that means *to be for*.

5. S-T-R-E-T-C-H: What is your favorite state? Write about it.

CONTEXT CLUES: INFORMATIONAL

Technology Over Time

Over time, technology changes and **evolves**. It gets smaller, faster, and usually less expensive. For example, the first computers were the size of an entire room. Yet, these early computers couldn't do very much. A modern laptop is faster and more powerful, plus it's **portable**. Forget about a computer that's the size of a room; you can carry a laptop from room to room. Or consider electronic calculators. The first ones were created in the 1960s. Only a few people could afford the $1,000 price tag for

the astonishing new invention. Today, a calculator can be purchased for a few dollars.

KEY QUESTIONS

1. CONTEXT CLUES: What do you think *evolves* means?

☐ stays the same ☐ develops over time
☐ goes backwards

2. TEXT EVIDENCE: What clues in the text helped you figure out the meaning of *evolves*?

3. WORD PARTS: The root *port* means "to carry." What do you think *portable* means?

☐ easily moved ☐ bolted down
☐ a place for boats

4. FUN FIND: Find a word in the text that means *amazing*.

5. S-T-R-E-T-C-H: Describe how an object or invention you use today might *evolve* in the future.

CONTEXT CLUES: INFORMATIONAL

Sensational Sumo Wrestling

Sumo wrestling is a big sport. It's big, as in the wrestlers are of **ample** size. Many weigh more than 500 pounds. It's also big, as in popular. Although this ancient sport started in Japan, people all over the world now watch it on TV. Two wrestlers meet in a ring. If one pushes the other out of the ring, he wins. A wrestler also wins if he can force his **opponent** to touch the ground with anything other than the soles of his feet. Say a huge Sumo wrestler momentarily loses his balance and quickly brushes his fingertips across the floor. Match over!

KEY QUESTIONS

1. CONTEXT CLUES: What do you think *ample* means?

☐ large ☐ tiny ☐ microscopic

2. TEXT EVIDENCE: What clues in the text helped you figure out the meaning of *ample*?

3. WORD PARTS: The prefix *op-* means "against." What do you think *opponent* means?

☐ partner or teammate
☐ rival or competitor
☐ mammal that plays dead

4. FUN FIND: Find a word in the text that means *for just an instant*.

5. S-T-R-E-T-C-H: What's your favorite sport? Describe some of the rules.

The World of Smells

When it comes to getting around every day, you probably don't rely much on your nose. Instead, you use your eyes and ears to **navigate** the world. Your sense of smell can come in handy, alerting you to things that are nice, like a fragrant rose, and not so nice, like a **malodorous** bag of garbage. But for much of the animal kingdom, the sense of smell plays a much bigger role. Bears, for example, use their sense of smell to find mates and track down food. And

elephants' sense of smell is so good that they can sniff out water a few miles away. Wow!

KEY QUESTIONS

1. CONTEXT CLUES: What do you think *navigate* means?

☐ smell ☐ get around ☐ listen to

2. TEXT EVIDENCE: What clues in the text helped you figure out the meaning of *navigate*?

3. WORD PARTS: The prefix *mal-* means "bad." What do you think *malodorous* means?

☐ important ☐ super-full ☐ stinky

4. FUN FIND: Find a word in the text that means *nice smelling*.

5. S-T-R-E-T-C-H: What are some smells you can quickly identify? Make a list and say whether you like them or not.

The Model T

The Model T is one of history's most significant inventions. The Ford Motor Company made the car during the early 1900s. It's one of the first items to be **mass-produced**. Workers assembled Model Ts in factories by the thousands. Model Ts were **affordable** (about $350) and nearly 15 million were sold. The cars had leather seats, headlights, and a horn. At first, Model Ts came in a choice of colors: green, blue, and red. But Ford started painting the cars only one color to make them more quickly at the factory. Between 1914 and 1926, Model Ts were available only in black.

KEY QUESTIONS

1. CONTEXT CLUES: What do you think *mass-produced* means?

☐ made in small batches
☐ made in large numbers
☐ made at night

2. TEXT EVIDENCE: What clues in the text helped you figure out the meaning of *mass-produced*?

3. WORD PARTS: The suffix *-able* can mean "capable of." What do you think *affordable* means?

☐ not too expensive ☐ expensive
☐ nice and shiny

4. FUN FIND: Find a word in the text that means *important*.

5. S-T-R-E-T-C-H: Can you think of more things that are *mass-produced*? Make a list.

Bottlenose Brainiacs

There are many species of dolphins, but maybe the most well-known is the bottlenose dolphin. Bottlenose dolphins are gray with short beaks, and they always appear to be smiling. And why not? They travel in large, playful groups known as pods. They avoid chilly waters, and instead they live in nice, **temperate** oceans. These **marine** mammals are also incredibly smart. They communicate with one another through their own language of clicking sounds, and they demonstrate many other signs of intelligence. In fact, some scientists think that the only creatures who are more intelligent than dolphins are humans.

KEY QUESTIONS

1. CONTEXT CLUES: What do you think *temperate* means?

☐ rocky   ☐ cold   ☐ not too cold or hot

2. TEXT EVIDENCE: What clues in the text helped you figure out the meaning of *temperate*?

3. WORD PARTS: The root *mar* means "the sea." What do you think *marine* means?

☐ blue
☐ related to the ocean
☐ talented

4. FUN FIND: Find a word in the text that means *show*.

5. S-T-R-E-T-C-H: Write two sentences. In one, use the word *temperate*. In the other, use the word *marine*.

Breads of the World

Bread is a **staple** in most diets around the world. But just as cultures around the world differ, so too does bread. In the United States and in many countries in Europe, bread comes baked in loaves. In India, people eat bread called naan, which is flat and round. In Middle Eastern countries, pita bread is popular. Pitas are round with a pouch in the middle that can be filled with meat or vegetables. In Mexico, people eat flat corn tortillas, which are the Mexican **equivalent** of bread. As you can see, bread can comprise many forms!

KEY QUESTIONS

1. CONTEXT CLUES: What do you think *staple* means?

☐ candy made from wheat
☐ very important item
☐ delicious treat

2. TEXT EVIDENCE: What clues in the text helped you figure out the meaning of *staple*?

3. WORD PARTS: The root *equi* means "equal." What do you think *equivalent* means?

☐ match   ☐ opposite   ☐ enemy

4. FUN FIND: Find a word in the text that means *to be made up of*.

5. S-T-R-E-T-C-H: Design an ad campaign for your favorite kind of bread.

What a Cool Job!

What's the coolest job ever? How about tasting ice cream for a living? Believe it or not, that's an actual job. At the ice cream company Ben and Jerry's, people are hired to be Flavor **Gurus**. These taste experts test lots of new ice cream flavors, and they also help create them. To do that, they go to shops and restaurants and taste a wide array of delicious foods. Then they try to come up with new ice cream flavors by **combining** different tastes. It sounds like a great job, but maybe even eating ice cream gets old after a while.

KEY QUESTIONS

1. CONTEXT CLUES: What do you think *gurus* means?

☐ testers ☐ experts ☐ cooks

2. TEXT EVIDENCE: What clues in the text helped you figure out the meaning of *gurus*?

3. WORD PARTS: The prefix *com-* means "with." What do you think *combining* means?

☐ tasting
☐ putting together
☐ scooping up

4. FUN FIND: Find a word in the text that means *assortment*.

5. S-T-R-E-T-C-H: What's your dream job? Tell why.

A Brief History of Brushing

The first toothbrushes were invented in China around 1500. **Initially**, toothbrushes had handles made of bamboo or bone and bristles made of short, stiff pig hair. What did people use for toothpaste? They mixed their own homemade **concoctions**. These were made of such items as crushed eggshells, mint leaves, and salt. During the 1800s, the first toothpastes started being sold commercially in stores. At first, toothpaste came in a jar. During the 1890s, toothpaste became available in tubes. Then, in 1927, the Electro Massage Tooth Brush company began producing and selling the first electric toothbrush. Hope this brief history of brushing made you smile!

KEY QUESTIONS

1. CONTEXT CLUES: What do you think *initially* means?

☐ at last ☐ at first
☐ to create fresh breath

2. TEXT EVIDENCE: What clues helped you figure out the meaning of *initially*?

3. WORD PARTS: The prefix *con-* can mean "with." What do you think *concoctions* means?

☐ treats
☐ vitamins
☐ combination of items

4. FUN FIND: Find a word in the text that means *sold in stores*.

5. S-T-R-E-T-C-H: Can you think of other words that use the prefix *con-*? Make a list!

Pickling to Preserve

Fresh food can go bad very quickly. Pickling is a way to **preserve** food, so it can be eaten later. Pickling is an ancient art. Before refrigerators existed, people had to figure out how to keep food around. So they stored food in liquids such as vinegar or salty water. Meats such as beef or pork can be pickled. It's possible to pickle **numerous** other foods, such as eggs, fish, fruits, and vegetables. Maybe you enjoy pickled cabbage. It's often known by its German name, *sauerkraut*. A popular food is pickled cucumbers. Pickled cucumbers are simply known as . . . pickles.

KEY QUESTIONS

1. CONTEXT CLUES: What do you think *preserve* means?

☐ season ☐ save ☐ get rid of

2. TEXT EVIDENCE: What clues in the text helped you figure out the meaning of *preserve*?

3. WORD PARTS: The root *numer* comes from "number." What do you think *numerous* means?

☐ a small number of
☐ an even number of
☐ a large number of

4. FUN FIND: Find a word in the text that means *very old*.

5. S-T-R-E-T-C-H: *Peter Piper picked a peck of pickled peppers* is a famous tongue twister. Write a new tongue twister about food.

Whistled Words

One of the world's most amazing languages is Silbo Gomero. The language is only used in parts of the Canary Islands. And it's only spoken—or rather, whistled—by about 22,000 people. That's right, Silbo Gomero is a language that features loud whistling. It was **practical** and quite useful in the old days, when most people worked outdoors as farmers and shepherds. The language was good for **conveying** messages over long distances. Loudly whistled words could be heard across valleys. Today, people can use cellphones to talk over great distances. Sadly, the ancient language of Silbo Gomero is in danger of becoming extinct.

KEY QUESTIONS

1. CONTEXT CLUES: What do you think *practical* means?

☐ uninteresting ☐ useful ☐ ridiculous

2. TEXT EVIDENCE: What clues in the text helped you figure out the meaning of *practical*?

3. WORD PARTS: The root *vey* means "to carry." What do you think *conveying* means?

☐ whistling loudly ☐ bringing
☐ forgetting

4. FUN FIND: Find a word in the text that means *gone forever*.

5. S-T-R-E-T-C-H: Silbo Gomero is a language in danger of extinction. Can you think of things that *have* become extinct? Make a list.

Mighty Elephants

The elephant is one of Earth's most amazing animals. For starters, there's the trunk. This strange **appendage** is roughly six feet long, and it functions as a nose and a hand. Elephants use their trunks to smell, scoop things up, grab objects, and more. This gigantic creature is also the world's largest land mammal. Adult males can weigh up to 16,000 pounds. That's eight tons! Somehow, they maintain their humongous size simply by eating plants and grass all day! Elephants are **herbivores**, so they don't eat other animals. They just eat grass, plants, and fruit. But then again, they do basically eat nonstop—12 to 18 hours a day.

KEY QUESTIONS

1. CONTEXT CLUES: What do you think *appendage* means?

- ☐ thing that covers cuts
- ☐ large land animal
- ☐ body part that sticks out

2. TEXT EVIDENCE: What clues in the text helped you figure out the meaning of *appendage*?

3. WORD PARTS: The root *vor* means "eat." What do you think *herbivore* means?

- ☐ animals that eat only plants
- ☐ animals that weigh a lot
- ☐ animals that scoop things

4. FUN FIND: Find two words in the text that mean *very large*.

5. S-T-R-E-T-C-H: Can you think of more synonyms for *large*? Make a list.

Shirley Temple, Child Star

Shirley Temple was one of the most popular child stars ever. She was bubbly and high-spirited. Moviegoers enjoyed her **exuberant** personality. Young Shirley appeared in her first movie at age 3. She became a big star in the 1930s during the Great Depression. That was a time when many Americans were dealing with high **unemployment**. Jobs were tough to find. Shirley Temple's carefree movies cheered people up. As a child, she starred in more than 20 films, including *Heidi*, *Curly Top*, and *The Little Princess*. She retired from movie making at the young age of 22.

KEY QUESTIONS

1. CONTEXT CLUES: What do you think *exuberant* means?

- ☐ dull and sad ☐ goofy and silly
- ☐ lively and energetic

2. TEXT EVIDENCE: What clues in the text helped you figure out the meaning of *exuberant*?

3. WORD PARTS: The suffix *-ment* means "a situation." What do you think *unemployment* means?

- ☐ jobless situation
- ☐ happy situation
- ☐ strange situation

4. FUN FIND: Find a word in the text that means *lacking in worry*.

5. S-T-R-E-T-C-H: Would you like to be a movie star? Tell why or why not.

Chill City

Yakutsk is the coldest big city in the world. It's in Russia. The average temperature is 16 degrees Fahrenheit. The coldest temperature ever recorded in Yakutsk was a **frigid** 84 degrees below zero. Only Antarctica has colder, harsher weather. But Antarctica doesn't have any large cities. In fact, it's almost **uninhabited**. Meanwhile, nearly 270,000 people live in chilly Yakutsk. There are stores and restaurants, and even two airports. During the very short summer, Yakutsk's populace puts on a big festival. The city also has a museum filled with exhibits about ice and cold weather. Would you like to live in Yakutsk?

KEY QUESTIONS

1. CONTEXT CLUES: What do you think *frigid* means?

☐ very warm ☐ extremely cold ☐ super-dark

2. TEXT EVIDENCE: What clues in the text helped you figure out the meaning of *frigid*?

3. WORD PARTS: The prefix *un-* means "not." What do you think *uninhabited* means?

☐ very cold ☐ not cold ☐ not lived in

4. FUN FIND: Find a word in the text that means *people.*

5. S-T-R-E-T-C-H: Would you like to live in Yakutsk? Write a paragraph telling why or why not.

A Switch Pitcher

Baseball pitchers are either righties or lefties. **Invariably**, they use that same hand to throw each pitch. Well, except Pat Venditte. He was the only **ambidextrous** pitcher in major-league baseball history. He could throw equally well with each hand. As a batter came to the plate, Venditte could choose to throw using his left or right hand. He also had a customized six-fingered glove. It had two thumbs. All Venditte had to do was flip the glove over, and he could wear it on either hand. Venditte spent four years in the big leagues and struck out 53 batters.

KEY QUESTIONS

1. CONTEXT CLUES: What do you think *invariably* means?

☐ in season ☐ always ☐ sometimes

2. TEXT EVIDENCE: What clues in the text helped you figure out the meaning of *invariably*?

3. WORD PARTS: The prefix *ambi-* means "both." What do you think *ambidextrous* means?

☐ both right-and left-handed
☐ frog-obsessed
☐ bilingual

4. FUN FIND: Find a word in the text that means *specially made.*

5. S-T-R-E-T-C-H: Write a paragraph in which you include the words *invariably* and *ambidextrous.*

An Oxy What?

Jumbo shrimp. A dull roar. Awfully good. These are all examples of a type of phrase called an **oxymoron**. They combine two words that are opposites. Take *jumbo shrimp*, for example. *Jumbo* means "big" and *shrimp* means "small." But even though *jumbo shrimp* seems like a **contradiction**, the phrase actually make sense. A shrimp is a little creature, but a jumbo shrimp is bigger than the standard variety. A roar is deafening, but a *dull roar* is just somewhat loud. These phrases show that you can be playful with words to get your point across. And if you put in some effort, you'll be able to do it terribly well!

KEY QUESTIONS

1. CONTEXT CLUES: What do you think *oxymoron* means?

☐ phrase that makes no sense
☐ phrase that makes you laugh
☐ phrase containing opposites

2. TEXT EVIDENCE: What clues in the text helped you figure out the meaning of *oxymoron*?

3. WORD PARTS: The prefix *contra-* means "against." What do you think *contradiction* means?

☐ saying of something funny
☐ saying of something opposite
☐ saying the truth

4. FUN FIND: Find a word in the text that means *very loud*.

5. S-T-R-E-T-C-H: Create your own oxymoron and use it in a sentence.

Hero of the Fields

The people who work in the fields to pick our fruits and vegetables do difficult work. Without these workers, we wouldn't have all the **produce** we eat—strawberries, corn, grapes, tomatoes, and other delicious foods that keep us healthy. These women and men work long hours under the hot sun, but they haven't always been treated fairly. In the 1960s, a woman named Dolores Huerta began to fight to ensure that these **agricultural** workers—many of whom were Mexican—were treated fairly. She helped get important laws passed to protect their rights. For many people, she was, and still is, a hero.

KEY QUESTIONS

1. CONTEXT CLUES: What do you think *produce* means?

☐ shoes and socks
☐ fruits and vegetables
☐ sky and fields

2. TEXT EVIDENCE: What clues in the text helped you figure out the meaning of *produce*?

3. WORD PARTS: The root *agri* means "field" or "soil." What do you think *agricultural* means?

☐ related to math ☐ related to music
☐ related to farming

4. FUN FIND: Find a word in the text that means *make sure*.

5. S-T-R-E-T-C-H: Who is one of your heroes? Write about that person.

CONTEXT CLUES: INFORMATIONAL

Leaning Tower of Pisa

Have you heard of the Leaning Tower of Pisa? It's a building in the Italian town of Pisa. It doesn't stand straight, as a proper tower should. Instead, it **tilts** to one side. Work on the tower began more than 800 years ago. The plan was bad from the beginning. The tower was built on very soft soil. By the time it reached its full eight-story height, the tower was precarious. In recent years, engineers have worked to **stabilize** the tower to keep it from leaning any more than it does. After all, it's one of the world's most famous attractions. Tourists love to see a tower that leans, but no one wants it to fall.

KEY QUESTIONS

1. CONTEXT CLUES: What do you think *tilts* means?

☐ straightens ☐ falls ☐ leans

2. TEXT EVIDENCE: What clues in the text helped you figure out the meaning of *tilts*?

3. WORD PARTS: The suffix *-ize* means "to make." What do you think *stabilize* means?

☐ make tall
☐ make fall down
☐ make secure

4. FUN FIND: Find a word in the text that means *dangerous* or *not safe*.

5. S-T-R-E-T-C-H: What is your favorite building? Write about it.

CONTEXT CLUES: INFORMATIONAL

Water Times Three

People think of water as something that fills a glass—or a bathtub. But water appears in the world in a **trio** of forms. Water can be a solid, a liquid, or a gas. So what is solid water? Simple: It's ice. When ice warms up, it melts and changes into water, the form that's familiar to everyone. But what happens if water keeps getting hotter? Well, think about a teapot sitting on the stove. When the water inside boils it **converts** from a liquid to a gas that's called steam. Steam rushes out of the teapot producing a whistling sound. Time for tea!

KEY QUESTIONS

1. CONTEXT CLUES: What do you think *trio* means?

☐ small tree ☐ pair ☐ set of three

2. TEXT EVIDENCE: What clues helped you figure out the meaning of *trio*?

3. WORD PARTS: The prefix *con-* can mean "completely." What do you think *converts* means?

☐ remains the same
☐ completely changes
☐ gets very hot

4. FUN FIND: Find a word in the text that means *making*.

5. S-T-R-E-T-C-H: What is your favorite form of water? Tell why.

The Power of the Sun

You already know that the sun is powerful. Although it's nearly 93 million miles away, the sun is so hot that it can keep you warm on a summer day, and even burn your skin. Plants **utilize** the

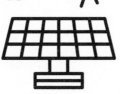

sun's great energy. They use it to grow. People use the sun's immense energy, too. We use it to create electricity. We build special panels that help turn the sun's energy into electricity. This form of power is called **solar** power, which means it comes from the sun. One day in the future, we might use the sun to drive cars, light up whole cities, and more!

KEY QUESTIONS

1. CONTEXT CLUES: What do you think *utilize* means?

☐ burn ☐ grow ☐ use

2. TEXT EVIDENCE: What clues in the text helped you figure out the meaning of *utilize*?

3. WORD PARTS: The root *sol* means "sun," What do you think *solar* means?

☐ related to plants
☐ related to energy
☐ related to the sun

4. FUN FIND: Find a word in the text that means *large and powerful*.

5. S-T-R-E-T-C-H: What are some other ways we experience the power of the sun? Write about it!

Awesome Alpacas

Alpacas live in South America. They are **domesticated** animals. Alpacas aren't wild animals like deer or antelope. In fact, they have been living with people for more than 5,000 years. Alpacas are related to camels and llamas, but they are smaller. Full-grown alpacas weigh about 150 pounds, equivalent to an adult person. Camels and llamas are often used by humans to **transport** heavy packs on their backs, but alpacas are raised for their fleece. Alpaca fleece is very soft. It's also waterproof and very warm. Alpaca fleece is perfect for sweaters and scarves.

KEY QUESTIONS

1. CONTEXT CLUES: What do you think *domesticated* means?

☐ wild ☐ tamed ☐ small

2. TEXT EVIDENCE: What clues in the text helped you figure out the meaning of *domesticated*?

3. WORD PARTS: The root *port* means "to carry." What do you think *transport* means?

☐ eat ☐ lift
☐ take from one place to another

4. FUN FIND: Find a word in the text that means *animal fur used in clothing and blankets*.

5. S-T-R-E-T-C-H: Write a summary of this passage.

Night Lights

Lucy and her family moved to Pennsylvania from California. This was her first summer in her new home state. One night after dinner, she hung out with her neighbor Sofia. They sat outside at **dusk**, when it was just getting dark. Suddenly, Lucy spotted a tiny yellow light in the newly dark air. The light grew bright and then **disappeared**. A minute later she saw another and another. She jumped up and yelled, "Look! Look!" Sofia chuckled at her friend. "There are so many fireflies," she said. "Ohhh!" Lucy said. "I've never seen one before."

KEY QUESTIONS

1. CONTEXT CLUES: What do you think *dusk* means?

☐ early morning
☐ the time just after sundown
☐ midnight

2. TEXT EVIDENCE: What clues in the text helped you figure out the meaning of *dusk*?

3. WORD PARTS: What do you think the prefix *dis-* means in the word *disappear*?

☐ not ☐ again ☐ before

4. FUN FIND: Find a word in the text that means *laughed*.

5. S-T-R-E-T-C-H: Another name for dusk is *twilight*. *Twi* means "two." Can you guess why *twilight* got its name?

Visitors From Planet Orange

Everything on Planet Orange was the same color. The sky, the sea, and every creature was orange. Three Orangeans decided to leave their **monochromatic** world to search for intelligent life on other planets. They boarded an orange spaceship (what else?) and traveled to Earth. Their ship **descended** into a grocery store parking lot. The aliens went inside. The shoppers were alarmed. But the orange aliens didn't seem to notice them. They wandered up and down the aisles stacked with many items. Finally, they stopped in front of a bin filled with oranges. "I knew it," said one alien. "This planet DOES have intelligent life."

KEY QUESTIONS

1. CONTEXT CLUES: What do you think *monochromatic* means?

☐ one color ☐ one sound ☐ shiny

2. TEXT EVIDENCE: What clues in the text helped you figure out the meaning of *monochromatic*?

3. WORD PARTS: The prefix *de-* means "down." What do you think *descended* means?

☐ spun in circles
☐ moved up
☐ moved down

4. FUN FIND: Find a word in the text that means *nervous and surprised*.

5. S-T-R-E-T-C-H: Write a mini-story about purple aliens from another planet.

Homemade Ice Cream

It was a **sweltering** day in July. To cool down, Emily decided to make ice cream. She mixed milk, cream, eggs, and sugar and poured the mixture into the bowl of the ice cream maker. The bowl was very cold, and the machine spun round and round, stirring the mixture. Slowly, the mixture became thicker and less liquid. After about 15 minutes it was good and thick. Now all it needed was a few hours in the freezer to completely **solidify**. That evening after dinner, Emily scooped up bowls of ice cream for her mom, dad, and brother. The ice cream was so scrumptious that they ate every last bit!

KEY QUESTIONS

1. CONTEXT CLUES: What do you think *sweltering* means?

☐ very hot ☐ sweet ☐ cold

2. TEXT EVIDENCE: What clues in the text helped you figure out the meaning of *sweltering*?

3. WORD PARTS: The suffix *-ify* means "to become." What do you think *solidify* means?

☐ become hot ☐ become cold
☐ become hard

4. FUN FIND: Find a word in the text that means *tasty*.

5. S-T-R-E-T-C-H: Have you ever made a yummy treat? Write about it.

Holiday Guest

When Jacob came home from school, he saw a giant spider sitting in a tank on the kitchen counter. His heart raced and he thought he might faint. His older sister Taylor came into the kitchen and said, "I see you met George. He's my class's pet tarantula. I'm taking care of him over the holidays." Jacob was **speechless**. He couldn't say a word. He just kept staring at the spider. "You look a little scared," Taylor said. "Don't tell me you have **arachnophobia**." Jacob shrugged. "As long as George stays in *your* room, everything will be dandy," he said.

KEY QUESTIONS

1. CONTEXT CLUES: What do you think *speechless* means?

☐ unable to talk ☐ very noisy
☐ very nervous

2. TEXT EVIDENCE: What clues in the text helped you figure out the meaning of *speechless*?

3. WORD PARTS: The root *phobia* means "fear of." What do you think *arachnophobia* means?

☐ a bad cold ☐ fear of heights
☐ fear of spiders

4. FUN FIND: Find a word in the text that means *great*.

5. S-T-R-E-T-C-H: Have you ever been speechless? What happened? Write about it!

CONTEXT CLUES: LITERARY

21st-Century Ant and Grasshopper

Ant and Grasshopper were friends at Insect High School. They were on summer break. Grasshopper **lounged** on the couch. He lazily stayed there for entire days, eating snacks and watching TV. Meanwhile, Ant got a job at Sugar Shack. "Skip work and watch TV with me," said Grasshopper. "I can't because I'm saving up for something cool," replied Ant. At summer's end, Ant and Grasshopper went to the mall. Ant bought a set of six tiny sneakers. Meanwhile, **impecunious** Grasshopper couldn't even afford a Buggy Blaster Super Soda. The moral of the story: It's best to prepare for the future.

KEY QUESTIONS

1. CONTEXT CLUES: What do you think *lounged* means?

- ☐ exercised ☐ worked hard
- ☐ lay around in a lazy way

2. TEXT EVIDENCE: What clues in the text helped you figure out the meaning of *lounged*?

3. WORD PARTS: The prefix *im-* means "without." What do you think *impecunious* means?

- ☐ has no friends ☐ has no money
- ☐ thirsty

4. FUN FIND: Find a word in the text that means *lesson*.

5. S-T-R-E-T-C-H: Come up with three adjectives to describe Ant and three to describe Grasshopper.

CONTEXT CLUES: LITERARY

Our Sick Tree

The great big tree in our front yard didn't look so good. Where before it looked healthy and **lush**—with nice full branches—it now appeared droopy and sparse. My dad called an **arborist**, hoping she could tell us what was wrong with our tree. She said our tree needed surgery! She said she needed to trim some of the diseased branches, and that in a few years, the tree would be healthy again. "A few years?" I said. "That seems like a long time." But she said that the tree would live more than a hundred years, so a few years was just a drop in the bucket.

KEY QUESTIONS

1. CONTEXT CLUES: What do you think *lush* means?

- ☐ full ☐ droopy ☐ bright

2. TEXT EVIDENCE: What clues in the text helped you figure out the meaning of *lush*?

3. WORD PARTS: The root *arbor* means "tree." What do you think *arborist* means?

- ☐ old tree ☐ ill tree
- ☐ expert who cares for trees

4. FUN FIND: Find a word in the text that means *sick*.

5. S-T-R-E-T-C-H: *A drop in the bucket* is an idiom. What do you think it means? Use it in a sentence of your own.

A One-Girl (Two-Pet) Band

Sandra started by quietly strumming her guitar. Soon, she added drums. She only had to tap on the pedal. *Boom, boom, boom!* **Simultaneously**, she blew into a kazoo. Sandra played all three instruments at once. She was a one-girl band. That's when her dog joined in. Duke threw back his head, and let out some sad, **mournful** howls. That caused the parrot to join in. "Polly want a cracker!" squawked the parrot. Then the phone rang. To Sandra, the ringing fit perfectly into her music. "It's Mrs. Alder, complaining," shouted her mother. "You have to stop making such a racket!" Sandra sighed and returned to strumming her guitar, quietly.

KEY QUESTIONS

1. CONTEXT CLUES: What do you think *simultaneously* means?

☐ at the same time ☐ with great skill
☐ loudly

2. TEXT EVIDENCE: What clues in the text helped you figure out the meaning of *simultaneously*?

3. WORD PARTS: The suffix *-ful* means "filled with." What do you think *mournful* means?

☐ without humor ☐ musical
☐ filled with sadness

4. FUN FIND: Find a word in the text that means *noisy disturbance*.

5. S-T-R-E-T-C-H: Sandra's one-girl band made quite a racket. Make a list of other things that "make a racket."

Cup of Sunshine

It was opening day for Lan's lemonade stand. The sky was dark and cloudy. "Too bad today is **overcast**," said Lan sadly. Lan sat and waited. Then she waited some more. Nobody seemed to be coming. She started to feel gloomy, kind of like the weather. She wondered if she was just no good at selling lemonade. She started to think about closing down her stand. But then something **unanticipated** happened. The sun broke through the clouds. The day grew warmer and warmer. Soon it was downright scorching. A long line of people formed, thirsty for lemonade. Lan's opening day was a big success!

KEY QUESTIONS

1. CONTEXT CLUES: What do you think *overcast* means?

☐ bright ☐ covered by a long coat
☐ cloudy and gray

2. TEXT EVIDENCE: What clues in the text helped you figure out the meaning of *overcast*?

3. WORD PARTS: The prefix *un-* means "not." What do you think *unanticipated* means?

☐ not lovable ☐ not expected
☐ not fun

4. FUN FIND: Find a word in the text that means *very hot*.

5. S-T-R-E-T-C-H: Imagine you're a weather person forecasting a cloudy day. Describe what you'd say.

The New Food in the Fridge

Inside the refrigerator, there were whispers in the dark. "Lila will pick me. I'm her favorite," said orange juice, confidently. Milk was **adamant**. Milk was sure *it* would be Lila's choice. But it had been there too long and had turned sour. Cottage cheese piped up. It was the new food in the fridge. "I'm not sure," said cottage cheese, "but I **surmise** she'll pick me." Suddenly, Lila opened the fridge door. She grabbed orange juice. Orange juice winked, telegraphing "I told you so" to the other foods. But then she set down orange juice and chose cottage cheese. In a tiny voice, cottage cheese said, "Yay!"

KEY QUESTIONS

1. CONTEXT CLUES: What do you think *adamant* means?

☐ certain ☐ unhappy ☐ sour

2. TEXT EVIDENCE: What clues in the text helped you figure out the meaning of *adamant*?

3. WORD PARTS: The prefix *sur-* means "upon." What do you think *surmise* means?

☐ have doubts ☐ insist ☐ guess

4. FUN FIND: Find a word in the text that means *sending a silent signal*.

5. S-T-R-E-T-C-H: What do you predict might happen next in this story? Write it!

Time for Sleep

Keenan couldn't fall asleep. This was **uncommon** for him. Usually, he got into bed and was asleep in five minutes. But tonight, he had **insomnia**. *Maybe I'm thirsty,* he thought. He went out to the kitchen and poured himself a glass of water. Then he climbed back into bed. But he was still awake. Maybe his room was too hot. He got up and opened a window. Maybe he needed a different pair of PJs. He changed into his favorites, which had stripes like a tiger. *Maybe I should just stop worrying about falling asleep,* he thought. So he stopped fretting. And soon he was fast asleep. *Zzzzzzz.*

KEY QUESTIONS

1. CONTEXT CLUES: What do you think *uncommon* means?

☐ not usual ☐ worrisome ☐ frequent

2. TEXT EVIDENCE: What clues in the text helped you figure out the meaning of *uncommon*?

3. WORD PARTS: The root *somnus* means "sleep." What do you think *insomnia* means?

☐ amazing dreams ☐ trouble sleeping
☐ a leg that fell asleep

4. FUN FIND: Find a word in the text that means *worrying*.

5. S-T-R-E-T-C-H: The root *ambul* means "walk" or "move." What do you think the word *somnambulate* means? Do you know anyone who does this?

The Big 100!

Today was a special day. Marta's great-grandmother was turning 100 years old. That will make her a **centenarian**! Marta's big family was coming from all over the place. Her cousins and aunts and great-aunts and uncles were all driving to Great Granny's house for the big celebration. Marta's mother ordered a huge cake from the best local bakery. When it was time, Marta put all 100 candles on the cake, and her dad lit them. Marta turned off the lights, and her father carried the cake out as everyone sang "Happy Birthday." As Great Granny made her special wish, her face was **illuminated** by all the candles. Then, everyone helped her blow them out!

KEY QUESTIONS

1. CONTEXT CLUES: What do you think *centenarian* means?

☐ 100-year-old
☐ adult
☐ grandmother

2. TEXT EVIDENCE: What clues in the text helped you figure out the meaning of *centenarian*?

3. WORD PARTS: The root *lumin* means "light." What do you think *illuminated* means?

☐ surprised ☐ smiling ☐ lit up

4. FUN FIND: Find a word in the text that means *nearby*.

5. S-T-R-E-T-C-H: What do you think Great Granny wished for? Write about it.

The Myth of King Midas

Long ago, there was a king named Midas who had a **passion** for gold. He loved gold more than anything. One day a god gave him a magic power: everything Midas touched would turn to gold. At first, the king was **euphoric**. Instantly, he had more gold than he had dreamed possible. But when he touched his food, it turned to gold and he couldn't eat. His glass of water turned to gold and he couldn't drink. And when he hugged his daughter, *she*  turned to gold. His wonderful gift was a curse, and he begged to have the power taken away. The god agreed and Midas's daughter was restored to life.

KEY QUESTIONS

1. CONTEXT CLUES: What do you think *passion* means?

☐ terrible fear
☐ great love
☐ mild interest

2. TEXT EVIDENCE: What clues in the text helped you figure out the meaning of *passion*?

3. WORD PARTS: The root *eu* means "good" or "well." What do you think *euphoric* means?

☐ scared ☐ sad ☐ happy

4. FUN FIND: Find a word in the text that means *returned*.

5. S-T-R-E-T-C-H: The myth of King Midas teaches a lesson. What do you think it is?

Natural Lighting

Liv was scared. She could not believe how dark it was inside the tent. *All tents should have nightlights* **installed**, she thought. *Nightlights should be built right into tents, like doors and windows.* Then she had an idea. After first grabbing an empty plastic water bottle, Liv crawled out of the tent. She used a tent spike to carefully poke some small holes in the bottle. Outside, fireflies swarmed in the night air. Liv ran around gathering them in her bottle. Then she returned to the tent. The little fireflies lit up, **emitting** a bright, warm glow. Liv had her nightlight. The next morning, she opened the bottle and set the fireflies free.

KEY QUESTIONS

1. CONTEXT CLUES: What do you think *installed* means?

☐ burned out ☐ built in ☐ lit up

2. TEXT EVIDENCE: What clues in the text helped you figure out the meaning of *installed*?

3. WORD PARTS: *Transmitting* means "sending along." What do you think *emitting* means?

☐ sending out
☐ moving in circles
☐ sending an email

4. FUN FIND: Find a word in the text that means *moved in large numbers.*

5. S-T-R-E-T-C-H: What is Liv's problem? How does she solve it?

House of Cards

Milo was building a house of cards. He knelt on the floor, focusing so hard that his tongue stuck out. It was **meticulous** work. The task required such care and patience. His cards kept falling, but he **persevered**. Eventually, Milo succeeded in building a little house of carefully stacked cards. He picked up his phone and snapped a picture. Then he set it back down. It was then that Milo received a call. The phone's vibrations caused the cards to tumble. *Oh well*, thought Milo, *at least I got a picture of my creation.*

KEY QUESTIONS

1. CONTEXT CLUES: What do you think *meticulous* means?

☐ careless and sloppy ☐ boring
☐ detailed and careful

2. TEXT EVIDENCE: What clues in the text helped you figure out the meaning of *meticulous*?

3. WORD PARTS: The root *severe* means "strict." What do you think *persevered* means?

☐ was strict about card tricks
☐ was strict about staying with a task
☐ was strict about making jam

4. FUN FIND: Find a word in the text that means *little shaking movements.*

5. S-T-R-E-T-C-H: What kind of person is Milo? Describe him in a few sentences.

The Tale of the Small Good Wolf

This is the tale of a very small wolf. He was about the size of a beagle. The wolf was far from **ferocious**. In fact, he was friendly and kind. He paid a visit to his neighbors, the Three Little Pigs. They lived in a strong, **durable** home made of bricks. He brought along board games and treats. He knocked on the door. Inside, he could hear the three pigs whispering. They were worried. "I think you are confusing me with my uncle, the Big Bad Wolf," he said. The pigs whispered some more. At last, they opened the door and invited the wolf inside. He and the pigs played checkers, gobbled treats, and had a tremendous time.

KEY QUESTIONS

1. CONTEXT CLUES: What do you think *ferocious* means?

☐ fierce and mean ☐ sweet and silly
☐ big and bouncy

2. TEXT EVIDENCE: What clues in the text helped you figure out the meaning of *ferocious*?

3. WORD PARTS: The prefix *dur-* means "hard." What do you think *durable* means?

☐ sturdy ☐ pretty ☐ dirty

4. FUN FIND: Find a word in the text that means *very great*.

5. S-T-R-E-T-C-H: Can you think of 10 words to describe the Small Good Wolf? Make a list.

Sunny Learns the Ropes

Arjun loved his new dog, Sunny, but she was in need of some training. Even though she was three years old, she was **disobedient**. She didn't sit when he told her to sit or come when he called her name. So Arjun and his mom took Sunny to dog training classes. The instructor helped them teach Sunny to sit, stay, and lie down. Every time Sunny did what she was supposed to, they rewarded her with a treat. Sunny loved treats! Before long, Sunny was doing everything right.
After eight weeks in class, she **graduated**. She even got the prize for the most obedient!

KEY QUESTIONS

1. CONTEXT CLUES: What do you think *disobedient* means?

☐ unfriendly ☐ badly behaved
☐ well behaved

2. TEXT EVIDENCE: What clues in the text helped you figure out the meaning of *disobedient*?

3. WORD PARTS: The root *grad* means "step" or "degree." What do you think *graduated* means?

☐ barked very loudly ☐ ate the treats
☐ finished school

4. FUN FIND: Find a word in the text that means *teacher*.

5. S-T-R-E-T-C-H: Write a paragraph about a pet. Use the words *disobedient* and *obedient*.

Just Like Old Times

It was summer and Keisha's big brother was home from college. Keisha had been looking forward to having him home, but now that he was here, she felt funny and **awkward** around him. He seemed so much older. He almost seemed like a different person! Just last summer, they hung out and played tennis at the neighborhood courts. But now, he was studying **philosophy**. He was reading big books about the meaning of life! For a few days, Keisha felt dejected. But one afternoon, Keisha saw her brother holding two rackets. "Hey little sis," he said. "Let's go play a game of tennis—just like old times."

KEY QUESTIONS

1. CONTEXT CLUES: What do you think *awkward* means?

☐ uncomfortable
☐ older
☐ comfortable

2. TEXT EVIDENCE: What clues in the text helped you figure out the meaning of *awkward*?

3. WORD PARTS: The root *soph* means "wise." What do you think *philosophy* means?

☐ big ideas ☐ sports ☐ math

4. FUN FIND: Find a word in the text that means *sad*.

5. S-T-R-E-T-C-H: Why do you think Keisha feels sad in the story? Write about it.

Time for a PJB

Joe sometimes watched his little brother and sister and made snacks for them. One of Joe's favorite foods was a PJB. Whenever Joe or his **siblings** got hungry, it was time for a PJB!

Joe was the inventor of this treat. Here are the **circumstances** that led to its creation. One time, Joe was in the mood for peanut butter and jelly. But there was no bread or even crackers in the house. However, there were some tortillas. So he spread peanut butter and jelly on a tortilla. Then, he rolled it up. It was delectable and easy to eat. Joe even came up with a cool name for his creation: PJB for "peanut butter and jelly burrito."

KEY QUESTIONS

1. CONTEXT CLUES: What do you think *siblings* means?

☐ mother and father
☐ brothers and sisters
☐ friends and foes

2. TEXT EVIDENCE: What clues in the text helped you figure out the meaning of *siblings*?

3. WORD PARTS: The prefix *circum-* means "around." What do you think *circumstances* means?

☐ big circles ☐ wheels
☐ the facts that surround an action

4. FUN FIND: Find a word in the text that means *very tasty*.

5. S-T-R-E-T-C-H: What odd snack do you like? Write about it.

The Spring Concert

Daria had the best singing voice in the middle school chorus. The music teacher praised her tone, and said it was the sweetest, most **melodious** voice in the group. When they were planning the spring concert, Daria was sure she would be assigned the big **solo**. She was so looking forward to singing a song all by herself. But a month before the concert, a girl named Beatrice joined the chorus. Some people said her voice was even *more* beautiful than Daria's! Daria was worried. Maybe she wouldn't get the big solo after all. However, the music teacher came up with a brilliant solution. Daria and Beatrice would sing a duet!

KEY QUESTIONS

1. CONTEXT CLUES: What do you think *melodious* means?

☐ loud   ☐ nice-sounding   ☐ squeaky

2. TEXT EVIDENCE: What clues in the text helped you figure out the meaning of *melodious*?

3. WORD PARTS: The root *solus* means "alone." What do you think *solo* means?

☐ song that rhymes
☐ slow song
☐ song sung alone

4. FUN FIND: Find a word in the text that means *very smart*.

5. S-T-R-E-T-C-H: What do you predict might happen next in the story? Write about it!

No More Hiccups

Myron had the hiccups. They did not go away as they normally did. They **persisted**. He went to school hiccupping, and he hiccupped through science and math. His friend Alonzo told him to hold his breath and count to 10. Still, Myron hiccupped. His friend Tina snuck up behind him and yelled, "Boo!" Still, Myron hiccupped. Myron did somersaults, bit into a tart lemon, stuck out his tongue. Nothing worked. Finally, the science teacher had a strategy that would **terminate** the hiccups for good: Drink a whole glass of water without taking a breath. Myron gave it a try and . . . no more hiccups!

KEY QUESTIONS

1. CONTEXT CLUES: What do you think *persisted* means?

☐ stopped happening   ☐ were silly
☐ kept going

2. TEXT EVIDENCE: What clues in the text helped you figure out the meaning of *persisted*?

3. WORD PARTS: The root *term* means "end." What do you think *terminate* means?

☐ whistle away   ☐ stop   ☐ cough

4. FUN FIND: Find a word in the text that means *sour*.

5. S-T-R-E-T-C-H: Have you ever had the hiccups? How did you make them go away?

CONTEXT CLUES: LITERARY

Mr. Whiskers

Amanda was on her way to have lunch with a friend when Mr. Whiskers, her cat, slipped out the door. He **bolted** onto the porch and down the front steps as fast as lightning. Mr. Whiskers had never been outside before, and Amanda was fearful that he would get lost. She **postponed** her lunch date and searched for Mr. Whiskers. She walked up one block and down the next. She spent two hours looking for him, calling his name. When she finally returned home, she was greeted by a glorious sight: Mr. Whiskers was sitting on the front porch, waiting for her to let him back inside.

KEY QUESTIONS

1. CONTEXT CLUES: What do you think *bolted* means?

☐ ran quickly ☐ skipped ☐ rolled

2. TEXT EVIDENCE: What clues in the text helped you figure out the meaning of *bolted*?

3. WORD PARTS: The prefix *post-* means "after." What do you think *postponed* means?

☐ called back ☐ went on
☐ changed to a later time

4. FUN FIND: Find a word in the text that means *wonderful*.

5. S-T-R-E-T-C-H: Think up as many synonyms as you can for *wonderful*. Then use them in a mini-story about an amazing cat

---

CONTEXT CLUES: LITERARY

The Greek Myth of Arachne

Arachne was a skilled **weaver**. She could spin thread to create the most beautiful cloth, more beautiful than anyone had ever seen. The goddess Athena believed that she herself was the best weaver, and she was jealous of Arachne. She challenged Arachne to a contest. They would both spin cloth, and they would ask the gods to decide whose cloth was better. After they'd both woven their cloth, the gods **proclaimed** that Arachne's was superior. Athena was so enraged that she turned Arachne into a spider. After that, Arachne spun webs instead of cloth for the rest of her days.

KEY QUESTIONS

1. CONTEXT CLUES: What do you think *weaver* means?

☐ maker of cloth
☐ spider
☐ Greek goddess

2. TEXT EVIDENCE: What clues in the text helped you figure out the meaning of *weaver*?

3. WORD PARTS: The root *claim* means "to say or call out." What do you think *proclaimed* means?

☐ wished ☐ announced ☐ chose

4. FUN FIND: Find a word in the text that means *better*.

5. S-T-R-E-T-C-H: Imagine a different ending to this myth. Now write it.

Best Vacation Ever

All her life, my grandmother wanted to go to Hawaii. Last summer, my mom and dad and I took her there. When we got off the plane, people handed us **garlands** of flowers, called "leis," to wear around our necks. Over the next week, we did a bunch of cool stuff. We hiked to a volcano and attended a luau, which is a Hawaiian feast. We also went snorkeling and saw all kinds of beautiful fish. Later, as we headed **homeward** on a plane, my grandmother declared: "I'm 75 years old, and that was the best vacation I've ever had!"

KEY QUESTIONS

1. CONTEXT CLUES: What do you think *garlands* means?

☐ Hawaiian food ☐ long plane rides
☐ strings or wreaths

2. TEXT EVIDENCE: What clues in the text helped you figure out the meaning of *garlands*?

3. WORD PARTS: The suffix *-ward* means "in the direction of." What do you think *homeward* means?

☐ away from home ☐ to a hotel
☐ toward home

4. FUN FIND: Find a word in the text that means *said*.

5. S-T-R-E-T-C-H: What was the best vacation you've ever had? Write about it.

A Perfect Autumn Day

Nerisa was in the park, trying to fly her kite. As she ran across an open field, the kite began to rise. Then it **abruptly** swerved. In an instant, it fell to the ground. Nerisa tried several more times. But her kite kept crashing. So she gave up. As she **departed** the park, she could hear the trees rustling. Her hair blew this way and that. It was almost as if the wind was sending her a message: *Try again.* Try again she did. This time, her kite flew high into the air . . . and stayed there, riding the breeze. What a perfect autumn day!

KEY QUESTIONS

1. CONTEXT CLUES: What do you think *abruptly* means?

☐ over time ☐ all of a sudden
☐ in slow motion

2. TEXT EVIDENCE: What clues in the text helped you figure out the meaning of *abruptly*?

3. WORD PARTS: The prefix *de-* can means "to separate." What do you think *departed* means?

☐ arrived at ☐ stayed at ☐ left

4. FUN FIND: Find a word in the text that means *making a soft sound*.

5. S-T-R-E-T-C-H: Imagine that the wind had a message for you. Create some dialogue between yourself and the wind.

Fitness Fans

Caleb's new teacher was a fitness **enthusiast**. She loved to exercise and stay fit. At the start of the year, she told Caleb's class that she was going to make sure everyone got lots of daily exercise. Caleb didn't like exercise. He wasn't strong, and he wasn't **flexible**. In fact, when he bent over, Caleb couldn't even touch his toes. His teacher told him not to worry. She said they would do just a little bit each day, and that everyone would be able to accomplish it. By the end of the year, Caleb could touch his toes and lift a heavy weight. Now he was enthusiastic about exercise, too!

KEY QUESTIONS

1. CONTEXT CLUES: What do you think *enthusiast* means?

☐ musician ☐ baseball player
☐ fan

2. TEXT EVIDENCE: What clues in the text helped you figure out the meaning of *enthusiast*?

3. WORD PARTS: The suffix *-ible* means "able." What do you think *flexible* means?

☐ able to lift weights ☐ able to eat
☐ able to bend easily

4. FUN FIND: Find a word in the text that means *carry through with something.*

5. S-T-R-E-T-C-H: What's your favorite way to exercise? Write about it.

Visit to a Country Cousin

The year was 1840. Ben, a city boy, visited his cousin, Eli. Eli lived in the country. The two enjoyed such **rural** pastimes as horseback riding and swimming in the creek. Eli also told Ben about the wild animals that lived in the woods nearby, including mountain lions. That night, Ben awoke with a start. A large shadow approached, one that looked exactly like a mountain lion. Ben grew **petrified**. "Eli," he croaked, pointing at the shadow. "It's just our cat, Jingles," replied Eli drowsily. Jingles hopped onto the bed and gave Ben a nuzzle. He relaxed. *This country living is different*, thought Ben, *but I like it.*

KEY QUESTIONS

1. CONTEXT CLUES: What do you think *rural* means?

☐ city-related ☐ country-related
☐ fun

2. TEXT EVIDENCE: What clues in the text helped you figure out the meaning of *rural*?

3. WORD PARTS: The root *petra* means "rock." What do you think *petrified* means?

☐ very funny ☐ very still with fear
☐ very loud

4. FUN FIND: Find a word in the text that means *sleepily.*

5. S-T-R-E-T-C-H: Do you prefer the city or the country? Why? Write about it.

Og the Artist

Og was a **unique** caveman. He was different from the others. Still, Og joined in a hunting **expedition**. The cavemen saw some deer. They all threw their spears, but missed. Well, all except Og. He was so busy looking at flowers that he didn't even throw his spear. When the cavemen returned home, they drew pictures on the cave wall. This was a way of explaining the day's events to the cave community. One caveman drew a deer. Another drew a spear. Og drew some flowers. "What mean, Og?" asked the other cavemen. "It just pretty picture," he answered. "Og artist."

KEY QUESTIONS

1. CONTEXT CLUES: What do you think *unique* means?

☐ one who speaks in grunts
☐ ordinary ☐ one of a kind

2. TEXT EVIDENCE: What clues in the text helped you figure out the meaning of *unique*?

3. WORD PARTS: The root *ped* means "foot." What do you think *expedition* means?

☐ journey ☐ walking stick
☐ foot massage

4. FUN FIND: Find a word in the text that means *a group that lives together*.

5. S-T-R-E-T-C-H: Cave-people dialogue is fun. Write some more.

Up in the Sky

Ji-woo loved looking up at the stars at night. When she grew up, she hoped to become an astronaut and **venture** to distant planets. Maybe one day she would visit Mars. For her birthday, Ji-woo's mom surprised her with a present: her very own **telescope**. Now she could look through the telescope to see the many stars and planets in our solar system. Ji-woo's mom also loved looking at stars, and on clear nights she pointed out the different constellations, or clusters of stars. Ji-woo's favorite constellation was Orion, which looks like a hunter shooting a bow and arrow!

KEY QUESTIONS

1. CONTEXT CLUES: What do you think *venture* means?

☐ go someplace far away ☐ study
☐ draw pictures about

2. TEXT EVIDENCE: What clues in the text helped you figure out the meaning of *venture*?

3. WORD PARTS: The prefix *tele-* means "far off." What do you think *telescope* means?

☐ tool to see things far away
☐ tool to see small things
☐ tool that records music

4. FUN FIND: Find a word in the text that means *groups of stars*.

5. S-T-R-E-T-C-H: Would you like to be an astronaut? Write about it.

The Little Tree

When Carmen was born her parents planted a tree in front of their house. It was just a **sapling**, a young tree with a slender trunk. Every year, as Carmen grew, so did the tree. The growth was so **gradual** that Carmen didn't notice it. When she was in fifth grade, her family moved to a different house across town. For many years, Carmen didn't see the tree. She went to high school and college. One day, she was in her old neighborhood and drove by her former house. What had happened to the little tree? It was huge! It had grown up, just like her.

KEY QUESTIONS

1. CONTEXT CLUES: What do you think *sapling* means?

☐ young tree   ☐ sticky substance
☐ bunch of flowers

2. TEXT EVIDENCE: What clues in the text helped you figure out the meaning of *sapling*?

3. WORD PARTS: The root *grad* means "step." What do you think *gradual* means?

☐ secret   ☐ little by little   ☐ sudden

4. FUN FIND: Find a word in the text that means *old* or *previous*.

5. S-T-R-E-T-C-H: What are some other things that happen gradually? Describe two or three.

Scarlett, the Circus Shrimp

Scarlett was **discontented** and down. She may have been a cleaner shrimp, but her real love was doing flips. She dreamed of being an acrobat. "We clean eel's teeth. That's what we do," said her mother. "Everyone in your shrimp family tree is a dentist," said her father. Scarlett paid no mind. She made friends with other reef creatures, such as a clownfish, a seahorse, and an octopus that liked to juggle. One day, Scarlett suddenly had a huge **inspiration**. Dentistry would not be her life's fate . . . showbiz would! Scarlett and her friends started the "Rip-Roaring Reef Circus." Scarlett loved the circus so much—she was one ecstatic shrimp!

KEY QUESTIONS

1. CONTEXT CLUES: What do you think *discontented* means?

☐ underwater   ☐ pleased   ☐ unhappy

2. TEXT EVIDENCE: What clues in the text helped you figure out the meaning of *discontented*?

3. WORD PARTS: The root *spir* means "to breathe in." What do you think *inspiration* means?

☐ creative burst   ☐ hopelessness
☐ silliness

4. FUN FIND: Find a word in the text that means *joyful*.

5. S-T-R-E-T-C-H: Dream up a sign for Scarlett's circus. Let *inspiration* strike you so that the sign will be lots of fun.

The New Neighbors

Bart was excited to see that a new family had moved in next door. He saw that the family had two children, a boy and a girl. Just by looking, he **estimated** that the boy was about his age. A few days later, his mother met the family and told Bart about them. She said the family had just moved to their town from Italy, and before that, they had lived in Sweden. Bart's mom said they were all **polyglots**. "What does that mean?" Bart asked. "They can speak Italian, Swedish, and English," his mom replied. Bart was amazed. He was eager to meet the new neighbors.

KEY QUESTIONS

1. CONTEXT CLUES: What do you think *estimated* means?

☐ guessed ☐ asked ☐ wondered

2. TEXT EVIDENCE: What clues in the text helped you figure out the meaning of *estimated*?

3. WORD PARTS: The prefix *poly-* means "many." What do you think *polyglots* means?

☐ people who speak several languages
☐ people from Sweden
☐ people who are new in town

4. FUN FIND: Find a word in the text that means *excited*.

5. S-T-R-E-T-C-H: What do you predict might happen next in this story? Write it!

The Beach Party

The first to arrive at the beach party was Tic-Tac-Toe. He was a giant toe. Soon Doe-Ray-Me showed up. She was a large, **disembodied** mouth with red lipstick. She just floated in the air, not part of a full person. Then La-Di-Da arrived. La-Di-Da was simply a nose. She pointed up toward the sky, comporting herself with great pride. La-Di-Da was **pretentious**. "I will only sniff the *very* best roses," she said. The beach party went just as one might expect. Tic-Tac-Toe busied himself drawing large x's and o's in the sand. Doe-Ray-Me sang sweet songs. And La-Di-Da sniffed in her stuck-up way at everything the other two did.

KEY QUESTIONS

1. CONTEXT CLUES: What do you think *disembodied* means?

☐ invisible
☐ large-bodied
☐ without a body

2. TEXT EVIDENCE: What clues in the text helped you figure out the meaning of *disembodied*?

3. WORD PARTS: The suffix *-ious* means "full of." What do you think *pretentious* means?

☐ full of rage ☐ full of self-importance
☐ full of love

4. FUN FIND: Find a word in the text that means *behaving*.

5. S-T-R-E-T-C-H: What happens next in the story? Write about it.

Glass Half Full, Glass Half Empty

Pete and Nate were late to dinner. Already, little Derek had drunk half of their glasses of chocolate milk. Derek was tricky that way. Maybe he thought his big brothers wouldn't notice if he drank only half. "My glass is still half full," said Nate. "I'm an **optimist**." He always saw the good in things. Nate happily drank the rest of his chocolate milk. "You saw your glass as half full," said Pete. "I see mine as half empty. I'm a pessimist." Pete stared at his glass and was **despondent**. So Nate grabbed Pete's glass and gulped down his brother's chocolate milk. "Good news! Your glass isn't half empty anymore," said Nate.

KEY QUESTIONS

1. CONTEXT CLUES: What do you think *optimist* means?

- [ ] person who fixes glasses
- [ ] person with a negative attitude
- [ ] person with a positive attitude

2. TEXT EVIDENCE: What clues in the text helped you figure out the meaning of *optimist*?

3. WORD PARTS: The prefix *de-* means "down." What do you think *despondent* means?

- [ ] falling down [ ] feeling down
- [ ] jumping down

4. FUN FIND: Find a word in the text that means *person with a negative attitude*.

5. S-T-R-E-T-C-H: Is it good to be an *optimist*? Write about it.

Sarcastic Shonda

You've heard of the boy who cried wolf. Shonda was the girl who used **sarcasm**. Everything she said was a joke, and actually meant the opposite. Shonda's sister wanted to play a game. "That sounds like a blast," Shonda said flatly. Her brother made a joke. "That's **hilarious**," she said, dryly. Then her father suggested going to Pizza Palace. This was Shonda's favorite restaurant. She REALLY wanted to go. So she said, "That sounds great." Her dad was livid. "If you don't want to go, you can just stay home," he replied angrily. That's when Shonda realized she needed to dial down her sarcasm.

KEY QUESTIONS

1. CONTEXT CLUES: What do you think *sarcasm* means?

- [ ] speaking in a sleepy way
- [ ] speaking in a cheerful way
- [ ] speaking in a mocking way

2. TEXT EVIDENCE: What clues in the text helped you figure out the meaning of *sarcasm*?

3. WORD PARTS: The suffix *-ous* can mean "filled with." What do you think *hilarious* means?

- [ ] serious [ ] very funny
- [ ] filled with loneliness

4. FUN FIND: Find a word in the text that means *extremely angry*.

5. S-T-R-E-T-C-H: Do you like sarcasm? Write about it.

The Old Checkers Game

Drew liked playing checkers with his brother, Paul. Unfortunately, the game was in **decrepit** condition. The set was old and the board was tattered. A lost black checker had been replaced with a black button. A penny passed for a red checker. Drew made a double jump. He hopped his penny over a black button and a brown bottle cap. "That bottle cap's your own piece," said Paul. "But it's brown," said Drew. "Brown is close in color to black." Paul replied: "Brown is also close to red." It was **bewildering**! "I know what I want for my birthday," said Drew. "A new checkers set."

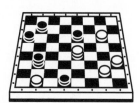

KEY QUESTIONS

1. CONTEXT CLUES: What do you think *decrepit* means?

☐ shiny and new ☐ worn out
☐ well preserved

2. TEXT EVIDENCE: What clues in the text helped you figure out the meaning of *decrepit*?

3. WORD PARTS: The prefix *be-* can mean "thoroughly." What do you think *bewildering* means?

☐ thoroughly brown
☐ thoroughly funny
☐ thoroughly confusing

4. FUN FIND: Find a word in the text that means *torn*.

5. S-T-R-E-T-C-H: Describe an object you own that's in *decrepit* condition.

(Almost) Perfect Priya

My friend Priya is the perfect friend. Well, *almost* perfect. In most ways, she's the **ideal** pal. She is fun and kind and is always on my side. We like to do the same things, and she's never boring. But she has this one habit that is a little annoying. She **interrupts** me when I'm talking. When I tell her about something that happened, she talks before I'm finished. Last week, I decided I'd had enough. I told her that she was the perfect friend, except for this one thing. She said she was sorry, and that she'd try to be more considerate—and she even waited until I was all done talking. You see? She's the best!

KEY QUESTIONS

1. CONTEXT CLUES: What do you think *ideal* means?

☐ imaginary ☐ perfect ☐ bossy

2. TEXT EVIDENCE: What clues in the text helped you figure out the meaning of *ideal*?

3. WORD PARTS: The root *rupt* means "break." What do you think *interrupts* means?

☐ breaks things on ☐ leaves
☐ speaks over

4. FUN FIND: Find a word in the text that means *thoughtful*.

5. S-T-R-E-T-C-H: What's Priya's problem? How does she solve it?

A Week of Vegetables

Oliver went to visit his aunt and uncle for a week. As soon as he arrived, he got some **disagreeable** news, which did not make him happy. His aunt and uncle were **vegetarians**. They didn't eat meat or fish. Oliver wasn't a fan of vegetables. He liked hotdogs and hamburgers and bacon and fried chicken. The only vegetable he really liked was French fries. *This is going to be a long week*, he thought. But in fact, his aunt and uncle were wonderful cooks. They made Mexican and Indian and Italian dishes. Every night was something new and delectable. Although Oliver still loved fried chicken, he discovered that vegetables weren't so bad after all.

KEY QUESTIONS

1. CONTEXT CLUES: What do you think *disagreeable* means?

☐ untrue ☐ bad or unpleasant
☐ exciting

2. TEXT EVIDENCE: What clues in the text helped you figure out the meaning of *disagreeable*?

3. WORD PARTS: The suffix *-arian* means "one who." What do you think *vegetarians* means?

☐ people who are good cooks
☐ people who hate vegetables
☐ people who eat only vegetables

4. FUN FIND: Find a word in the text that means *good-tasting*.

5. S-T-R-E-T-C-H: Write about a meatless meal you had that you really liked.

Envelope Man Saves the Day

Envelope Man was a **humdrum** superhero. He was boring and lacked special powers like flight and X-ray vision. Basically, he was just an envelope with tiny arms and legs. Then, one day, he was ambling down the street, simply minding his own sad superhero business. "Oh, no," cried a woman. "I locked my keys inside my house." This was an **extraordinary** opportunity. Envelope Man sprang into action. He slipped into the woman's house through a mail slot in the door. He located her keys. Then he slipped back out, and presented the keys. "My hero!" said the woman. Envelope Man blushed with pride, turning from white to pink.

KEY QUESTIONS

1. CONTEXT CLUES: What do you think *humdrum* means?

☐ dull ☐ exciting ☐ powerful

2. TEXT EVIDENCE: What clues in the text helped you figure out the meaning of *humdrum*?

3. WORD PARTS: The prefix *extra-* means "beyond." What do you think *extraordinary* means?

☐ extremely boring ☐ extremely odd
☐ extremely great

4. FUN FIND: Find a word in the text that means *walking in a slow, relaxed way*.

5. S-T-R-E-T-C-H: Dream up an *extraordinary* superhero and describe his or her powers.

Wendy the Magnificent!

Wendy was an ordinary girl. She did all the **typical** things kids her age did. She went to school, read lots of books, and played with her friends. But in her imagination, Wendy had all kinds of marvelous adventures. She was a lion tamer at the circus, fearlessly putting her head in a lion's mouth. She was an astronaut who took trips to outer space and saw stars and planets. She rode a **unicycle** down the sidewalk while juggling flaming torches. She went deep-sea diving and scaled Mount Everest. With every new book, Wendy had a new adventure. Best of all, when she was done, she went to sleep in her own bed!

KEY QUESTIONS

1. CONTEXT CLUES: What do you think *typical* means?

☐ imaginary ☐ extraordinary
☐ usual

2. TEXT EVIDENCE: What clues in the text helped you figure out the meaning of *typical*?

3. WORD PARTS: The prefix *uni-* means "one." What do you think *unicycle* means?

☐ very large bike ☐ juggler
☐ bicycle with one wheel

4. FUN FIND: Find a word in the text that means *climbed*.

5. S-T-R-E-T-C-H: List five things you would do, if you could do anything at all.

An Awesome Day

For Jamal's birthday, his dad got two tickets to the baseball game. Jamal was a baseball **fanatic**! He loved the game, and he watched it on TV whenever he could. He hadn't been to many games, so this was a special treat. His dad arranged to get there early so they could watch batting practice. Jamal brought his glove, and when a ball came into the stands he caught it. What a thrill! Then the outfielder saw Jamal, and he came over and **autographed** the ball. Jamal's dad high-fived him. "Wow," Jamal said. "The game hasn't even started yet, and this day is already awesome!"

KEY QUESTIONS

1. CONTEXT CLUES: What do you think *fanatic* means?

☐ huge fan ☐ player ☐ ticket

2. TEXT EVIDENCE: What clues in the text helped you figure out the meaning of *fanatic*?

3. WORD PARTS: The root *graph* means "write." What do you think *autographed* means?

☐ told a story of one's life ☐ threw
☐ signed

4. FUN FIND: Find a word in the text that means *planned*.

5. S-T-R-E-T-C-H: Whose autograph would you like to have? Tell why.

A Lot to Learn

Miguel got the lead in the school play. He loved acting, and he'd really wanted the part. Now he worried about how gargantuan the role was! He needed to **memorize** *a lot* of lines. He would have to read them over and over until they stuck in his head. There was even a **monologue** that he would have to perform on stage all by himself. Miguel briefly thought about quitting, but it was too late for that. So he got his little sister to help him with his lines, and pretty soon, he knew them forwards and backwards. He was ready. He couldn't wait for the big night!

KEY QUESTIONS

1. CONTEXT CLUES: What do you think *memorize* means?

☐ act on stage ☐ forget
☐ learn by heart

2. TEXT EVIDENCE: What clues in the text helped you figure out the meaning of *memorize*?

3. WORD PARTS: The prefix *mono-* means "one." What do you think *monologue* means?

☐ lot of lines ☐ difficult role
☐ speech by one actor

4. FUN FIND: Find a word in the text that means *huge*.

5. S-T-R-E-T-C-H: How do you think Miguel would have felt if he'd quit the play? Tell why.

A Clean Dirt Bike

Max had a brand-new red dirt bike. "Honestly, it's even faster than your bike," he told Mindy. "I can do cooler tricks, too." Mindy didn't like Max's habit of bragging. She found it **irritating**. The two were on a road that led to the base of a hill. There was no more road—just a steep, dirt **incline**. "Well, I'm off," said Mindy. She set off riding up the bumpy hillside. When she reached the top, she saw that Max hadn't moved. "Aren't you coming up to join me?" yelled Mindy. "I don't want to get my new dirt bike, uh, dirty," Max sheepishly answered.

KEY QUESTIONS

1. CONTEXT CLUES: What do you think *irritating* means?

☐ annoying ☐ fabulous ☐ fast-moving

2. TEXT EVIDENCE: What clues in the text helped you figure out the meaning of *irritating*?

3. WORD PARTS: The root *cline* means "to lean." What do you think *incline* means?

☐ sidewalk ☐ lake ☐ slope

4. FUN FIND: Find a word in the text that means *with embarrassment*.

5. S-T-R-E-T-C-H: Write a paragraph on the topic of your choice. In it, use the words *irritating*, *incline*, and *sheepishly*.

Up Off the Couch

Jake's dad decided to run a **marathon**. The race was 26.2 miles from start to finish. There was only one problem. Jake's dad was a couch potato. He hadn't run in years, and these days he hardly ever walked. Jake gave his dad a **pedometer** to track his steps and told him to start with 10,000 steps a day. After a few months, Jake and his dad went on short runs, just a mile or two. Slowly his dad increased his distance. It took him a year, but eventually he was ready for the marathon. He didn't run fast, but he finished! Jake was so proud of his father.

KEY QUESTIONS

1. CONTEXT CLUES: What do you think *marathon* means?

☐ very long race ☐ parade
☐ short race

2. TEXT EVIDENCE: What clues in the text helped you figure out the meaning of *marathon*?

3. WORD PARTS: The root *meter* means "measure." What do you think *pedometer* means?

☐ thing that helps one run far
☐ thing that counts steps
☐ 10,000 steps

4. FUN FIND: Find a word in the text that means *after a time*.

5. S-T-R-E-T-C-H: How do you think Jake's dad felt at the end of the race?

Where's Yertle?

When Lucy's pet turtle, Yertle, went missing, she was **puzzled**. She had no idea how he had gotten out of the tank. She couldn't figure out where he could be. Everyone in the family took a room and carefully **inspected** it. After searching the entire apartment, they still hadn't found Yertle. A day went by, then another and another. After a week, Lucy wondered if Yertle had gotten outside and left for eternity. But then she was sitting on the sofa and she felt something move beneath the pillow. She lifted the pillow and there was Yertle, safe and sound!

KEY QUESTIONS

1. CONTEXT CLUES: What do you think *puzzled* means?

☐ afraid ☐ confused ☐ angry

2. TEXT EVIDENCE: What clues in the text helped you figure out the meaning of *puzzled*?

3. WORD PARTS: The root *spect* means "look" or "see." What do you think *inspected* means?

☐ ran after ☐ examined closely
☐ found

4. FUN FIND: Find a word in the text that means *forever*.

5. S-T-R-E-T-C-H: Imagine a different ending to this story. Now write it!

Temper-Tantrum Taco and Tina

As Tina prepared to take a bite of her taco, the shell began to talk. Tina was flabbergasted. She couldn't **discern** what the taco was saying. Its voice was hard to hear because it was stuffed with fixings. Then the **furious** taco shell spit out the ground beef, tomatoes, and cheese. The fixings flew everywhere. "Don't you dare eat me!" it shouted. Of course, Tina wasn't about to eat a talking taco, even one

that was throwing a fit. That's how *Temper-Tantrum Taco and Tina* became one of the biggest internet shows.

KEY QUESTIONS

1. CONTEXT CLUES: What do you think *discern* means?

☐ confuse ☐ understand
☐ agree with

2. TEXT EVIDENCE: What clues in the text helped you figure out the meaning of *discern*?

3. WORD PARTS: The suffix *-ious* means "filled with." What do you think *furious* means?

☐ filled with joy ☐ covered in fur
☐ filled with anger

4. FUN FIND: Find a word in the text that means *greatly surprised*.

5. S-T-R-E-T-C-H: Write an episode of *Temper-Tantrum Taco and Tina*.

Trader Joel

Joel sat down to lunch. He had a turkey and cheese sandwich on white bread. But Joel liked to make trades. "That bagel sure looks good," said Joel to Debbie. "I'll trade you my bread for it." Debbie made the trade. Joel **scanned** the lunch table. He noticed that Javier had beef stew. "I'll trade you turkey for stew," he said. Javier made the trade. Joel managed one more **exchange** with Rory, swapping his cheese for pickle slices. Joel assembled his various lunch items. He now had a bagel with beef stew and pickles. Joel took a bite. *Mmmm,* not bad at all!

KEY QUESTIONS

1. CONTEXT CLUES: What do you think *scanned* means?

☐ tricked ☐ looked carefully
☐ tasted carefully

2. TEXT EVIDENCE: What clues in the text helped you figure out the meaning of *scanned*?

3. WORD PARTS: The prefix *ex-* can mean "out." What do you think *exchange* means?

☐ purchase ☐ discard ☐ swap

4. FUN FIND: Find a word in the text that means *put together*.

5. S-T-R-E-T-C-H: Trading a bike for a gumball would be an unfair exchange. Describe a fair exchange.

Hand-Me-Down Sweater

Elle received a pink sweater for her birthday. She frowned. It was a gift from her aunt, whom she hadn't seen in several years. Pink happened to be a color Elle **detested**. She loved blue. So she handed the sweater down to her little sister, Gwen. Gwen adored pink. Gwen washed the sweater and it shrank. So Gwen handed the sweater down to the youngest sister, Traci. Now the sweater's yarn was loose. The sweater began to **unravel**. So Traci handed the sweater *up* to her grandmother, who used the loose yarn to knit a brand-new sweater!

KEY QUESTIONS

1. CONTEXT CLUES: What do you think *detested* means?

☐ strongly disliked
☐ liked to give others
☐ appreciated greatly

2. TEXT EVIDENCE: What clues in the text helped you figure out the meaning of *detested*?

3. WORD PARTS: The prefix *un-* means "not." What do you think *unravel* means?

☐ come apart   ☐ stick together
☐ grow larger

4. FUN FIND: Find a word in the text that means *loved deeply*.

5. S-T-R-E-T-C-H: List some items that you used to *detest* but have come to like.

Pan Pizza

Peter claimed to have a magic pan. The pan could turn into a pizza. "Could you **bestow** some dough?" he asked Jayla. Jayla gave him some dough. Peter spread it in the pan. "Sauce would be boss," he said to Nick. Nick gave him sauce. Peter slathered it onto the dough. "Cheese, please," he said to Gabi. Gabi provided cheese. Peter sprinkled it over the sauce. Next, Peter popped the pan in the oven. Twenty minutes **elapsed**, then he pulled it out. Everyone was amazed. The magic pan had turned into a pizza!

KEY QUESTIONS

1. CONTEXT CLUES: What do you think *bestow* means?

☐ take   ☐ steal   ☐ give

2. TEXT EVIDENCE: What clues in the text helped you figure out the meaning of *bestow*?

3. WORD PARTS: The root *lapse* means "to slip." What do you think *elapsed* means?

☐ slipped by   ☐ baked   ☐ fell

4. FUN FIND: Find a word in the text that means *spread*.

5. S-T-R-E-T-C-H: What would you put on your dream pizza? Write about it.

Cheering Is Tiring, Too

Ozzy was at the big football game. He wore a shirt with the name of his favorite player. He proudly waved a **pennant** for the team. Ozzy even painted his face the team colors. Whenever the crowd **erupted** in cheering, Ozzy joined in. Whenever the crowd did the wave, Ozzy jumped to his feet. The game was very exciting and very close. His team won, 27–24. "I'm so worn out," Ozzy announced when he arrived home. "But you didn't play," said his mother. "You only watched." That was true. Simply watching had been exhausting. Ozzy brushed his teeth, washed off his face paint, and went to bed.

KEY QUESTIONS

1. CONTEXT CLUES: What do you think *pennant* means?

☐ a championship ring ☐ a wallet
☐ a flag

2. TEXT EVIDENCE: What clues in the text helped you figure out the meaning of *pennant*?

3. WORD PARTS: The root *rupt* means "break." What do you think *erupted* means?

☐ broke, as in no money ☐ broke out
☐ broke in half

4. FUN FIND: Find a word in the text that means *very tiring*.

5. S-T-R-E-T-C-H: Are you a big sports fan? Why or why not?

Too-Cool Pool

Jazmín's friends were in the pool, swimming and splashing. She waded in slowly, until the water reached her tummy. *Brrrr!* How could her friends be enjoying this too-cool pool? "You just have to go under," shouted Mira. "Try counting to three," offered Halle helpfully. "1 . . . 2 . . . 3." But Jazmín just stood there, **immobile**, waist-deep in the water. Finally, she inched forward. Suddenly, she lost her balance, and found herself **submerged**. For a moment, she felt shockingly cold. But she quickly grew acclimated, and the water felt just fine. Soon, Jazmín was swimming and splashing and having fun with her friends.

KEY QUESTIONS

1. CONTEXT CLUES: What do you think *immobile* means?

☐ cold ☐ warm ☐ motionless

2. TEXT EVIDENCE: What clues in the text helped you figure out the meaning of *immobile*?

3. WORD PARTS: The prefix *sub-* means "below." What do you think *submerged* means?

☐ above the water ☐ below the water
☐ below the cold

4. FUN FIND: Find a word in the text that means *became used to new conditions*.

5. S-T-R-E-T-C-H: Provide instructions for getting used to the temperature of the water in a swimming pool.

INFORMATIONAL

All About Bats (Card 1)

1. *Nocturnal* means "active at night."
2. The passage says, "They sleep during the day, hanging upside down." It also says, "They are very busy at night."
3. *Omnivores* means "animals that eat plants and animals."
4. *Emerge* means "to come out of."
5. Answers will vary.

Hungry Dads! (Card 2)

1. *Abstaining from* means "going without."
2. The passage says, "Imagine abstaining from food for two whole months! That's how long male emperor penguins go without eating."
3. *Liberated* means "released."
4. *Secure* means "safe."
5. Answers will vary.

What's in a Name? (Card 3)

1. *Acclaimed* means "well known and loved."
2. The passage says, "People the world over applaud and praise his funny stories."
3. *Pseudonym* means "pretend name."
4. *Pleasurable* means "enjoyable."
5. Answers will vary.

The Curse of Spring (Card 4)

1. *Elated* means "happy."
2. The passage says, "They are happy that the weather is warmer, the snow has melted, and the flowers are in bloom."
3. *Rhinitis* means "irritated nose."
4. *Vivid* means "colorful and bright."
5. Answers will vary.

Our Planets (Card 5)

1. *Rotate* means "move around."
2. The passage says, "These eight planets all rotate around our sun."
3. *Demoted* means "lowered."
4. *Content* means "happy."
5. Answers will vary.

Mosquitoes in the Rain (Card 6)

1. *Diminutive* means "very small."
2. The passage says, "A single raindrop can be 50 times their size!"
3. *Evade* means "get away from."
4. *Plummets* means "fall quickly."
5. Answers will vary.

Ahoy or Hello? (Card 7)

1. *Greeting* means "word of welcome."
2. The passage says, "They didn't know what to say to start a conversation."
3. *Preferable* means "to be better."
4. *Convinced* means "to be sure of something."
5. Answers will vary.

No Ropes (Card 8)

1. *Boulders* means "large rocks."
2. The passage says, "Maybe you've climbed over big rocks or boulders while on a hike."
3. *Ascend* means "climb up."
4. *Expertise* means "skill."
5. Answers will vary.

Bubblegum Inventor (Card 9)

1. *Expand* means "become larger."
2. The passage says, "It needed to blow up like a balloon, getting bigger and bigger."
3. *Reinvent* means "invent again."
4. *Formula* means "list of ingredients."
5. Answers will vary.

Amazing Hummingbirds (Card 10)

1. *Hover* means "fly in the same place."
2. The passage says, "They can hover in the air, staying in the same spot, as if they're treading water in midair."
3. *Maximum* means "most amount."
4. *Rapid* means "fast."
5. Answers will vary.

Pyramids Are Everywhere (Card 11)

1. *Structure* means "building."
2. The passage says, "Throughout history, people have built pyramids in many different places."
3. *Beloved* means "very loved."
4. *Ubiquitous* means "everywhere."
5. Answers will vary.

World Cup Winners (Card 12)

1. *Dominant* means "the most powerful."
2. The passage says, "The U.S. team had been dominant, winning four out of the first eight World Cup tournaments."
3. *Undisputed* means "not challenged."
4. *Consecutive* means "back-to-back."
5. Answers will vary.

Sensational Sea Otters (Card 13)

1. *Reside* means "live."
2. The passage says, "Instead, they live in shallow, icy waters, such as the northern Pacific Ocean."
3. *Ingesting* means "taking in."
4. *Shallow* means "not very deep."
5. Answers will vary.

Life-Saving Mold! (Card 14)

1. *Visualize* means "picture in your mind."
2. The passage says, "You picture slimy, green fungus growing on bread or a piece of fruit."
3. *Antibiotic* means "medicine that kills germs."
4. *Foe* means "enemy."
5. Answers will vary.

1, 2, 3 . . . Googol! (Card 15)

1. *Infinite* means "going forever."
2. The passage says, "But you wouldn't have to stop there, because numbers are infinite—they never end."
3. *Unfathomably* means "impossible to grasp."
4. *Ceaselessly* means "without stopping."
5. Answers will vary.

Madame Doctor (Card 16)

1. *Occupation* means "job."
2. The passage says, "Women were expected to work in jobs like teachers, nannies, or cooks."
3. *Excluded from* means "not let in."
4. *Physicians* means "doctors."
5. Answers will vary.

Good Enough to Eat? (Card 17)

1. *Deceiving* means "untrue."
2. The passage says, "What you see in photos isn't always real. Food photographers use lots of tricks."
3. *Gastronomy* means "good cooking."
4. *Genuine* means "real."
5. Answers will vary.

It All Started With *Bertie the Brain* (Card 18)

1. *Elementary* means "easy."
2. The passage says, "The first video game was created in 1950. It was called *Bertie the Brain,* and it was very elementary—just a simple game of tic-tac-toe."
3. *Enormous* means "larger than normal."
4. *Breakthrough* means "important change."
5. Answers will vary.

Are You Superstitious? (Card 19)

1. *Skittish* means "fearful."
2. The passage says, "Some people are skittish of black cats. Others are afraid to walk under ladders."
3. *Beneficial* means "favorable."
4. *Dodge* means "avoid."
5. Answers will vary.

What Is the Moon? (Card 20)

1. *Orbit* means "circle around."
2. The passage says, "Moons orbit planets, going around and around them.
3. *Astronomers* means "scientists who study space."
4. *Myriad* means "a very large number of."
5. Answers will vary.

Arctic Giant (Card 21)

1. *Massive* means "large and heavy."
2. The passage says, "These massive creatures can weigh as much as 1,500 pounds. They maintain their large size with a carnivorous diet."
3. *Carnivorous* means "meat-eating."
4. *Decrease* means "lessen."
5. Answers will vary.

So Many Microbes! (Card 22)

1. *Approximate* means "close but not exact."
2. The passage says, "The exact number varies from one person to the next, but experts say an approximate number is 37 trillion."
3. *Microbes* means "small living things."
4. *Infinitesimal* means "very tiny."
5. Answers will vary.

Why People Say "Pencil Lead" (Card 23)

1. *Device* means "tool."
2. The passage says, "The ancient Romans had a very useful tool called a stylus."
3. *Forerunner* means "thing that came before."
4. *Encasing* means "covering and surrounding."
5. Answers will vary.

Big World, Small Countries (Card 24)

1. *Minuscule* means "tiny."
2. The passage says, "Our huge world has some very small countries. Monaco is minuscule, covering less than one square mile. The entire country is about the size of a very small town."
3. *Annually* means "every year."
4. *Secreted* means "hidden."
5. Answers will vary.

A New Name for Starfish (Card 25)

1. *Accurate* means "correct."
2. The passage says, "These incredible creatures used to be known as 'starfish.' But experts realized that name wasn't accurate, because these creatures aren't actually fish at all."
3. *Regenerate* means "grow back."
4. *Limb* means "arm or leg."
5. Answers will vary.

Who's #8? (Card 26)
1. *Overlooked* means "ignored."
2. The passage says, "Other presidents, such as George Washington and Abraham Lincoln, get more attention."
3. *Tireless* means "without losing energy."
4. *Primary* means "first."
5. Answers will vary.

Not Only a Good Writer (Card 27)
1. *Accomplished* means "successful."
2. The passage says, "She's the author of the wildly popular Harry Potter series of books, which have been translated into 60 different languages. The series has sold more than 400 million copies."
3. *Humanitarian* means "person who cares about people."
4. *Opted* means "chosen."
5. Answers will vary.

A Horse Nap (Card 28)
1. *Predator* means "animal that eats other animals."
2. The passage says, "The benefit of sleeping while standing up is clear. If a predator comes along that wants to eat them, horses can run away quickly if they're already on their feet."
3. *Alternate* means "change."
4. *Capacity* means "ability."
5. Answers will vary.

Deserts, Hot and Cold (Card 29)
1. *Precipitation* means "rain and snow."
2. The passage says, "A desert is a place that gets very low precipitation, less than 10 inches of rain or snow per year."
3. *Classified as* means "put together with."
4. *Harsh* means "difficult or intense."
5. Answers will vary.

The 51st State? (Card 30)
1. *Territory* means "area of land."
2. The passage says, "That means it is part of the United States, but it does not have all the rights and benefits that the 50 states have."
3. *Statehood* means "being a state."
4. *Support* means "to be for."
5. Answers will vary.

Technology Over Time (Card 31)
1. *Evolves* means "develops over time."
2. The passage says, "Over time, technology changes and evolves."
3. *Portable* means "easily moved."
4. *Astonishing* means "amazing."
5. Answers will vary.

Sensational Sumo Wrestling (Card 32)
1. *Ample* means "large."
2. The passage says, "Many weigh more than 500 pounds."
3. *Opponent* means "rival or competitor."
4. *Momentarily* means "for just an instant."
5. Answers will vary.

The World of Smells (Card 33)
1. *Navigate* means "get around."
2. The passage says, "When it comes to getting around every day, you probably don't rely much on your nose. Instead, you use your eyes and ears to navigate the world."
3. *Malodorous* means "stinky."
4. *Fragrant* means "nice smelling."
5. Answers will vary.

The Model T (Card 34)

1. *Mass-produced* means "made in large numbers."
2. The passage says, "Workers assembled Model Ts in factories by the thousands."
3. *Affordable* means "not too expensive."
4. *Significant* means "important."
5. Answers will vary.

Bottlenose Brainiacs (Card 35)

1. *Temperate* means "not too cold or hot."
2. The passage says, "They avoid chilly waters, and instead they live in nice, temperate oceans."
3. *Marine* means "related to the ocean."
4. *Demonstrate* means "show."
5. Answers will vary.

Breads of the World (Card 36)

1. *Staple* means "very important item."
2. The passage includes different kinds of bread from all over the world.
3. *Equivalent* means "match."
4. *Comprise* means "to be made up of."
5. Answers will vary.

What a Cool Job! (Card 37)

1. *Gurus* means "experts."
2. The passage says, "At the ice cream company Ben and Jerry's, people are hired to be Flavor Gurus. These taste experts test lots of new ice cream flavors, and they also help create them."
3. *Combining* means "putting together."
4. *Array* means "assortment."
5. Answers will vary.

A Brief History of Brushing (Card 38)

1. *Initially* means "at first."
2. The passage says, "The first toothbrushes were invented in China around 1500."
3. *Concoctions* means "combination of items."
4. *Commercially* means "sold in stores."
5. Answers will vary.

Pickling to Preserve (Card 39)

1. *Preserve* means "save."
2. The passage says, "Pickling is a way to preserve food, so it can be eaten later."
3. *Numerous* means "a large number of."
4. *Ancient* means "very old."
5. Answers will vary.

Whistled Words (Card 40)

1. *Practical* means "useful."
2. The passage says, "It was practical and quite useful in the old days."
3. *Conveying* means "bringing."
4. *Extinct* means "gone forever."
5. Answers will vary.

Mighty Elephants (Card 41)

1. *Appendage* means "body part that sticks out."
2. The passage says, "This strange appendage is roughly six feet long, and it functions as a nose and a hand."
3. *Herbivore* means "animals that eat only plants."
4. *Gigantic* and *humongous* mean "very large."
5. Answers will vary.

Shirley Temple, Child Star (Card 42)

1. *Exuberant* means "lively and energetic."
2. The passage says, "She was bubbly and high-spirited."
3. *Unemployment* means "jobless situation."
4. *Carefree* means "lacking in worry."
5. Answers will vary.

Chill City (Card 43)

1. *Frigid* means "extremely cold."
2. The passage says, "Yakutsk is the coldest big city in the world. Only Antarctica has colder, harsher weather."
3. *Uninhabited* means "not lived in."
4. *Populace* means "people."
5. Answers will vary.

A Switch Pitcher (Card 44)

1. *Invariably* means "always."
2. The passage says, "Invariably, they use that same hand to throw each pitch."
3. *Ambidextrous* means "both right- and left-handed."
4. *Customized* means "specially made."
5. Answers will vary.

An Oxy What? (Card 45)

1. *Oxymoron* means "phrase containing opposites."
2. The passage says, "They combine two words that are opposites."
3. *Contradiction* means "saying of something opposite."
4. *Deafening* means "very loud."
5. Answers will vary.

Hero of the Fields (Card 46)

1. *Produce* means "fruits and vegetables."
2. The passage says, "Without these workers, we wouldn't have all the produce we eat—strawberries, corn, grapes, tomatoes, and other delicious foods that keep us healthy."
3. *Agricultural* means "related to farming."
4. *Ensure* means "make sure."
5. Answers will vary.

Leaning Tower of Pisa (Card 47)

1. *Tilts* means "leans."
2. The passage says, "It doesn't stand straight, as a proper tower should."
3. *Stabilize* means "make secure."
4. *Precarious* means "dangerous" or "not safe."
5. Answers will vary.

Water Times Three (Card 48)

1. *Trio* means "set of three."
2. The passage says, "Water can be a solid, a liquid, or a gas."
3. *Converts* means "completely changes."
4. *Producing* means "making."
5. Answers will vary.

The Power of the Sun (Card 49)

1. *Utilize* means "use."
2. The passage says, "Plants utilize the sun's great energy. They use it to grow."
3. *Solar* means "related to the sun."
4. *Immense* means "large and powerful."
5. Answers will vary.

Awesome Alpacas (Card 50)

1. *Domesticated* means "tamed."
2. The passage says, "Alpacas aren't wild animals like deer or antelope."
3. *Transport* means "take from one place to another."
4. *Fleece* means "animal fur used in clothing and blankets."
5. Answers will vary.

LITERARY

Night Lights (Card 51)

1. *Dusk* means "the time just after sundown."
2. The passage says, "They sat outside at dusk, when it was just getting dark."
3. *Dis-* means "not."
4. *Chuckled* means "laughed."
5. Answers will vary.

Visitors From Planet Orange (Card 52)

1. *Monochromatic* means "one color."
2. The passage says, "Everything on Planet Orange was the same color. The sky, the sea, and every creature was orange."
3. *Descended* means "moved down."
4. *Alarmed* means "nervous and surprised."
5. Answers will vary.

Homemade Ice Cream (Card 53)

1. *Sweltering* means "very hot."
2. The passage says, "It was a sweltering day in July. To cool down, Emily decided to make ice cream."
3. *Solidify* means "become hard."
4. *Scrumptious* means "tasty."
5. Answers will vary.

Holiday Guest (Card 54)

1. *Speechless* means "unable to talk."
2. The passage says, "He couldn't say a word."
3. *Arachnophobia* means "fear of spiders."
4. *Dandy* means "great."
5. Answers will vary.

21st-Century Ant and Grasshopper (Card 55)

1. *Lounged* means "lay around in a lazy way."
2. The passage says, "He lazily stayed there for entire days eating snacks and watching TV."
3. *Impecunious* means "has no money."
4. *Moral* means "lesson."
5. Answers will vary.

Our Sick Tree (Card 56)

1. *Lush* means "full."
2. The passage says, "Where before it looked healthy and lush—with nice full branches—it now appeared droopy and sparse."
3. *Arborist* means "expert who cares for trees."
4. *Diseased* means "sick."
5. Answers will vary.

A One-Girl (Two-Pet) Band (Card 57)

1. *Simultaneously* means "at the same time."
2. The passage says, "Sandra played all three instruments at once."
3. *Mournful* means "with sadness."
4. *Racket* means "noisy disturbance."
5. Answers will vary.

Cup of Sunshine (Card 58)
1. *Overcast* means "cloudy and gray."
2. The passage says, "The sky was dark and cloudy."
3. *Unanticipated* means "not expected."
4. *Scorching* means "very hot."
5. Answers will vary.

The New Food in the Fridge (Card 59)
1. *Adamant* means "certain."
2. The passage says, "Milk was sure *it* would be Lila's choice."
3. *Surmise* means "guess."
4. *Telegraphing* means "sending a silent signal."
5. Answers will vary.

Time for Sleep (Card 60)
1. *Uncommon* means "not usual."
2. The passage says, "Usually he got into bed and was asleep in five minutes."
3. *Insomnia* means "trouble sleeping."
4. *Fretting* means "worrying."
5. *Somnabulate* means "sleepwalk." The rest of the answer will vary.

The Big 100! (Card 61)
1. *Centenarian* means "a 100-year-old."
2. The passage says, "Marta's great-grandmother was turning 100 years old. That will make her a centenarian!"
3. *Illuminated* means "lit up."
4. *Local* means "nearby."
5. Answers will vary.

The Myth of King Midas (Card 62)
1. *Passion* means "great love."
2. The passage says, "He loved gold more than anything."
3. *Euphoric* means "happy."
4. *Restored* means "returned."
5. Answers will vary.

Natural Lighting (Card 63)
1. *Installed* means "built in."
2. The passage says, "Nightlights should be built right into tents, like doors and windows."
3. *Emitting* means "sending out."
4. *Swarmed* means "moved in large numbers."
5. Answers will vary.

House of Cards (Card 64)
1. *Meticulous* means "detailed and careful."
2. The passage says, "The task required such care and patience."
3. *Persevered* means "was strict about staying with a task."
4. *Vibrations* means "little shaking movements."
5. Answers will vary.

The Tale of the Small Good Wolf (Card 65)
1. *Ferocious* means "fierce and mean."
2. The passage says, "The wolf was far from ferocious. In fact, he was friendly and kind."
3. *Durable* means "sturdy."
4. *Tremendous* means "very great."
5. Answers will vary.

Sunny Learns the Ropes (Card 66)
1. *Disobedient* means "badly behaved."
2. The passage says, "She didn't sit when he told her to sit or come when he called her name."
3. *Graduated* means "finished school."
4. *Instructor* means "teacher."
5. Answers will vary.

Just Like Old Times (Card 67)

1. *Awkward* means "uncomfortable."
2. The passage says, "She felt funny and awkward around him."
3. *Philosophy* means "big ideas."
4. *Dejected* means "sad."
5. Answers will vary.

Time for a PJB (Card 68)

1. *Siblings* means "brothers and sisters."
2. The passage says, "Joe sometimes watched his little brother and sister and made snacks for them."
3. *Circumstances* means "facts that surround an action."
4. *Delectable* means "very tasty."
5. Answers will vary.

The Spring Concert (Card 69)

1. *Melodious* means "nice-sounding."
2. The passage says, "Daria had the best singing voice in the middle school chorus" and "The music teacher praised her tone, and said it was the sweetest, most melodious voice in the group."
3. *Solo* means "song sung alone."
4. *Brilliant* means "very smart."
5. Answers will vary.

No More Hiccups (Card 70)

1. *Persisted* means "kept going."
2. The passage says, "They did not go away as they normally did. They persisted."
3. *Terminate* means "stop."
4. *Tart* means "sour."
5. Answers will vary.

Mr. Whiskers (Card 71)

1. *Bolted* means "ran quickly."
2. The passage says, "He bolted onto the porch and ran down the front steps as fast as lightning."
3. *Postponed* means "changed to a later time."
4. *Glorious* means "wonderful."
5. Answers will vary.

The Greek Myth of Arachne (Card 72)

1. *Weaver* means "maker of cloth."
2. The passage says, "She could spin thread to create the most beautiful cloth, more beautiful than anyone had ever seen."
3. *Proclaimed* means "announced."
4. *Superior* means "better."
5. Answers will vary.

Best Vacation Ever (Card 73)

1. *Garlands* means "strings or wreaths."
2. The passage says, "When we got off the plane, people handed us garlands of flowers, called 'leis,' to wear around our necks."
3. *Homeward* means "toward home."
4. *Declared* means "said."
5. Answers will vary.

A Perfect Autumn Day (Card 74)

1. *Abruptly* means "all of a sudden."
2. The passage says, "In an instant, it fell to the ground."
3. *Departed* means "left."
4. *Rustling* means "making a soft sound."
5. Answers will vary.

Fitness Fans (Card 75)
1. *Enthusiast* means "fan."
2. The passage says, "She loved to exercise and stay fit."
3. *Flexible* means "able to bend easily."
4. *Accomplish* means "carry through with something."
5. Answers will vary.

Visit to a Country Cousin (Card 76)
1. *Rural* means "country-related."
2. The passage says, "Eli lived in the country."
3. *Petrified* means "very still with fear."
4. *Drowsily* means "sleepily."
5. Answers will vary.

Og the Artist (Card 77)
1. *Unique* means "one of a kind."
2. The passage says, "He was different from the others."
3. *Expedition* means "journey."
4. *Community* means "group that lives together."
5. Answers will vary.

Up in the Sky (Card 78)
1. *Venture* means "go someplace far away."
2. The passage says, "When she grew up, she hoped to become an astronaut and venture to distant planets."
3. *Telescope* means "tool to see things far away."
4. *Constellations* means "groups of stars."
5. Answers will vary.

The Little Tree (Card 79)
1. *Sapling* means "young tree."
2. The passage says, "It was just a sapling, a young tree with a slender trunk."
3. *Gradual* means "little by little."
4. *Former* means "old" or "previous."
5. Answers will vary.

Scarlett, the Circus Shrimp (Card 80)
1. *Discontented* means "unhappy."
2. The passage says, "Scarlett was discontented and down. She may have been a cleaner shrimp, but her real love was doing flips."
3. *Inspiration* means "creative burst."
4. *Ecstatic* means "joyful."
5. Answers will vary.

The New Neighbors (Card 81)
1. *Estimated* means "guessed."
2. The passage says, "Just by looking, he estimated that the boy was about his age."
3. *Polyglots* means "people who speak several languages."
4. *Eager* means "excited."
5. Answers will vary.

The Beach Party (Card 82)
1. *Disembodied* means "without a body."
2. The passage says, "She just floated in the air, not part of a full person."
3. *Pretentious* means "full of self-importance."
4. *Comporting* means "behaving."
5. Answers will vary.

Glass Half Full, Glass Half Empty (Card 83)
1. *Optimist* means "a person with a positive attitude."
2. The passage says, "He always saw the good in things."
3. *Despondent* means "feeling down."
4. *Pessimist* means "person with a negative attitude."
5. Answers will vary.

Sarcastic Shonda (Card 84)

1. *Sarcasm* means "speaking in a mocking way."
2. The passage says, "Everything she said was a joke, and actually meant the opposite."
3. *Hilarious* means "very funny."
4. *Livid* means "extremely angry."
5. Answers will vary.

The Old Checkers Game (Card 85)

1. *Decrepit* means "worn out."
2. The passage says, "The set was old and the board was tattered. A lost black checker had been replaced with a black button."
3. *Bewildering* means "thoroughly confusing."
4. *Tattered* means "torn."
5. Answers will vary.

(Almost) Perfect Priya (Card 86)

1. *Ideal* means "perfect."
2. The passage says, "My friend Priya is the perfect friend. Well, *almost* perfect."
3. *Interrupts* means "speaks over."
4. *Considerate* means "thoughtful."
5. Answers will vary.

A Week of Vegetables (Card 87)

1. *Disagreeable* means "bad or unpleasant."
2. The passage says, "As soon as he arrived, he got some disagreeable news, which did not make him happy."
3. *Vegetarians* means "people who eat only vegetables."
4. *Delectable* means "good-tasting."
5. Answers will vary.

Envelope Man Saves the Day (Card 88)

1. *Humdrum* means "dull."
2. The passage says, "He was boring and lacked special powers like flight and X-ray vision."
3. *Extraordinary* means "extremely great."
4. *Ambling* means "walking in a slow, relaxed way."
5. Answers will vary.

Wendy the Magnificent! (Card 89)

1. *Typical* means "usual."
2. The passage says, "Wendy was an ordinary girl."
3. *Unicycle* means "bicycle with one wheel."
4. *Scaled* means "climbed."
5. Answers will vary.

An Awesome Day (Card 90)

1. *Fanatic* means "huge fan."
2. The passage says, "He loved the game, and he watched it on TV whenever he could."
3. *Autographed* means "signed."
4. *Arranged* means "planned."
5. Answers will vary.

A Lot to Learn (Card 91)

1. *Memorize* means "learn by heart."
2. The passage says, "He would have to read them over and over until they stuck in his head."
3. *Monologue* means "speech by one actor."
4. *Gargantuan* means "huge."
5. Answer will vary.

A Clean Dirt Bike (Card 92)

1. *Irritating* means "annoying."
2. The passage says, "Mindy didn't like Max's habit of bragging."
3. *Incline* means "slope."
4. *Sheepishly* means "with embarrassment."
5. Answers will vary.

Up Off the Couch (Card 93)

1. *Marathon* means "very long race."
2. The passage says, "The race was 26.2 miles from start to finish."
3. *Pedometer* means "thing that counts steps."
4. *Eventually* means "after a time."
5. Answers will vary.

Where's Yertle? (Card 94)

1. *Puzzled* means "confused."
2. The passage says, "She had no idea how he had gotten out of the tank. She couldn't figure out where he could be."
3. *Inspected* means "examined closely."
4. *Eternity* means "forever."
5. Answers will vary.

Temper-Tantrum Taco and Tina (Card 95)

1. *Discern* means "understand."
2. The passage says, "Its voice was hard to hear because it was stuffed with fixings."
3. *Furious* means "filled with anger."
4. *Flabbergasted* means "greatly surprised."
5. Answers will vary.

Trader Joel (Card 96)

1. *Scanned* means "looked carefully at."
2. The passage says, "He noticed that Javier had beef stew."
3. *Exchange* means "swap."
4. *Assembled* means "put together."
5. Answers will vary.

Hand-Me-Down Sweater (Card 97)

1. *Detested* means "strongly disliked."
2. The passage says, "She frowned" and "Pink happened to be a color Elle detested. She loved blue."
3. *Unravel* means "come apart."
4. *Adored* means "loved deeply."
5. Answers will vary.

Pan Pizza (Card 98)

1. *Bestow* means "give."
2. The passage says, "Jayla gave him some dough."
3. *Elapsed* means "slipped by."
4. *Slathered* means "spread."
5. Answers will vary.

Cheering Is Tiring, Too (Card 99)

1. *Pennant* means "a flag."
2. The passage says, "He proudly waved a pennant for the team."
3. *Erupted* means "broke out."
4. *Exhausting* means "very tiring."
5. Answers will vary.

Too-Cool Pool (Card 100)

1. *Immobile* means "motionless."
2. The passage says, "But Jazmín just stood there, immobile, waist-deep in the water."
3. *Submerged* means "below the water."
4. *Acclimated* means "became used to new conditions."
5. Answers will vary.

Notes

Notes